Coda & Riffs
Two Plays

Coda & Riffs

Two Plays
by
Bill Harris

Broadside Press - Detroit

Copyright © 1990 by Bill Harris
All Rights Reserved
First Edition

ACKNOWLEDGMENTS

Publication of this book was made possible through the support of:

    THE MICHIGAN COUNCIL FOR THE ARTS AND CULTURAL AFFAIRS
    &
    THE ARTS LEAGUE OF MICHIGAN

SPECIAL THANKS TO:

Cover Design by Kevin Davidson
Typesetting/Content Design by Charles R. Alexander

CAUTION: These plays are fully protected, in whole, in part, or in any form under the copyright laws of the United States of America and all other countries of the copyright union, and are subject to royalty. All rights, including professional, amateur, motion picture, radio, television, recitation, public reading, are strictly reserved. All inquiries for performance rights must be addressed to the author:
Bill Harris, 667 West Bethune Detroit, Michigan 48220

ISBN: 0-940713-12-8

Broadside Press — Detroit

To Blackmen who have walked the walk and talked the talk, but have not had their stories told.

"I love the rhythm in a riff."
BILLY ECKSTEIN

AUTHOR'S NOTE:

Your home is like an ancestor, a relative. You love it because it shaped you, and no matter what it or you become, you remember it through young eyes—when it was its sharpest, its hippest, its happiest—and/or if its present image is flaking, charred or down at the heels due to internal or external neglect, or the places you loved are no longer physically there, they remain, nevertheless, in your memory and heart, like that wedding or graduation-day photo. And you love it anyway. Detroit is my home.

Charlie Parker, or "Bird," as he was nicknamed, one of the finest jazz saxophonists ever, was one of the prime developers of Bebop. He was the era's most influential personality, epitomizing both musically and stylistically the daring and innovative period.

Contents

Coda 11
Riffs 139

CODA

Coda: a concluding musical section at the end of a composition, introduced to bring it to a satisfactory close.

> "When you have to explore every night, even the most beautiful things become the most painful."
> BOBBY HUTCHERSON

Coda

Coda opened April 27, 1990, at the Attic Theatre in Detroit, Michigan, with the following cast:

MADDOX (DOX) .... Von H. Washington
WEATHERSPOON (SPOON) .... Booker Hinton
ROYST .... Wayne David Parker
THERESA .... Judy Milner

Tenor Saxophone .... Thomas "Beans" Bowles
Bass .... Ray McKinney

Director: Woodie King, Jr.
Set and Costume Design: Felix E. Cochren
Light Design: Paul Epton
Music Director: Thomas "Beans" Bowles
Sound Design: Jim Lillie & Bill Smitka
Production Stage Manager: Patricia Ansuini

The final monologue, SPOON'S curtain speech, has been previously published in *Voices of color: 50 Scenes and Monologues by African American Playwrights,* Edited by Woodie King, Jr., Applause Books, and *Arts Midwest JazzLetter,* Spring 1992, Vol. 10 No. 2

Coda

CHARACTERS

MADDOX (DOX)   Late forties. Black. Jazz musician.

WEATHERSPOON   (SPOON) late forties. Black. Bar owner.

ROYST   Late thirties, early forties. White. Former musician, now host of children's television program. Huck Finn in Pat Boone's clothing.

THERESA   Early twenties. Black. Daughter of Maddox. Jazz musician. Has hard edged, hip sense of humor. Never self-pitying.

SETTING

North-End Detroit neighborhood jazz club (Spoon's Lounge) should have the feeling of being lighted primarily by the sunlight which fights its way in from outside & the few neon signs & working lights behind the bar; not gloomy but dim. There is possibly a mural featuring a declining, scantily clad female, or dueling horn players, on the wall behind the bandstand. Also publicity photos, some yellowing and curling, of musicians who have worked the club over the years. A piano on the bandstand. Small tables with chairs, seat down atop them.

TIME

Monday, March 14, 1955, morning

ACT ONE

(We hear a tenor saxophone playing a blues with a big, Gene Ammons or Ben Webster-like sound. We discover DOX as he finishes dressing. He is in a dark, cell-like area. Bar-like shadows fall across him. Even here we notice his sense of dignity and bemused tolerance of the significant and insignificant things of the world. He is holding a tenor saxophone. Blues continue as light fades on DOX.
Light up on SPOON in the bar; plays at intervals throughout.)

SPOON

This joint featured shake dancers when I started tending bar here. I changed it to an all jazz policy soon as I owned it, even through there was already music everywhere you turned in Detroit—before, during and after hours. Little girls jumping rope to *Now's The Time*. Mamas doing their shopping and grannies fanning to *Groovin' High*. Bar-b-quing, shoe shining, hair frying and dying, making love and raising kids to *Hot House* and *'Round About Midnight*. Henry Ford was turning out automobiles in River Rouge and Dearborn and we were turning out music on the North End. Good times.

I hired Dox to bring a band in. (He's my brother in law. Not that that was the reason.) We married the former Park sisters, me, Paulette and him, Lily. Paulette was a shake dancer working right in here when I met her. (Chick ain't shook nothing but her finger since we been married. I think she considered herself retired from the minute we said "Glad to meet you.") And Dox, like I say, married Lily, rest her soul. Lily was a piano player.

(Pause)

Anyway, '48 or '49, he brought a group in, including Lily on piano. I thought just for a week or so, just to see how it would go. It turned into like the first two years of an orgy of great f'ing jazz.

Every night cats getting their degrees in Jazzology, taught by the local masters: Dox, Billy Mitchell, Barry . . . Have to get a gun and make the cats come down off the stand. The joint, him, Lily, the music, me, we all got pretty well known. Nationally even. You come to Detroit, you come to Spoon's; Diz, Bird, Pres, Bean, Bud, Max, Monk, and you go away raving about the joint and the music. Got some pretty nice write ups, too. <u>Down Beat</u>, <u>Metronome</u>, far away as <u>Music Maker</u> in England, even.

Yeah, everybody just jamming and having a ball, Dox as much as anybody.

Till Lily died of a brain hemorrhage.

(Snaps his fingers. "Just that suddenly.")
And it all ended for Dox. He just got to be a glutton for alcohol. Over night looked like. He could always drink, but not like to *punish* himself with it.

(Shakes his head at the thought of it.)
And then it looked like drinking wasn't quick enough and he got deep in drugs. Paulette and me kept Theresa, him and Lily's daughter. And he ended up getting busted in Chicago and going to jail. The whole thing just a crying shame.

DOX
(Has completed his dressing. He is sharp, but not rigidly so. "Cell bars" fade. He looks around one last time, then, with horn in case, moves to bar. He stops before entering. Gets himself together.

> SPOON *is reading paper or doing bartending busy-work.*
>
> DOX *enters.*
>
> *They look at each other, seemingly without recognition or acknowledgment.* DOX *very deliberately looks around, then, mock serious.)*

So this is Spoon's Lounge; where all them Motor City jazz musicians play?

SPOON
You writing a book, or casing the joint, junior?

DOX
Ain't nothing in here worth stealing, *mon homme*. And I don't hear no music.

SPOON
This is a *night*club, Negro. It's 10 o'clock in the morning. You in violation of the law just being in here.

> *(Referring to instrument case.)*

And what's that, your luggage?

DOX
You mighty nosey for a bartender.

SPOON
I know, I bet you it's a saxophone. You learn to play *Ornithology* yet, or don't your mama 'low you to listen to Bebop, Jug Blower?

DOX
I could play it when your mama first whistled it for me—bartender.

SPOON
You don't want to get into the dozens with me, junior.

DOX
Who you, colored boy, I got to tip toe 'round the dozens 'round you?

SPOON
Captain Dozens, far as you concerned.

DOX
(Scats Ornithology. SPOON and DOX drop all pretense and greet each other: obviously two old friends who have not seen each other for far too long. They are equals in each others eyes. Each having respect for who the other is and the way in which he does the work he does. At every opportunity they laugh at each others jokes out of familiarity and the genuine joy of being together.)

SPOON
(Indicating horn. This is a part of a familiar ritual.)
When you get so you can do that with that stove pipe in your mouth, then you'll be doing something.

DOX
It's a miracle you had sense enough to hire somebody good as me to play in this hole in the wall. Paulette must've pulled your coat.

SPOON
You mighty cocky for a jailbird, Negro. And you best get that hipster tone out your voice when you addressing me, or I'll have you back on that chain gang so quick it'll make your head swim.

(*Laughs. They slap palms.*)

DOX
(*Avoiding embarrassed sincerity.*)
Thanks for the clothes, Spoon.

SPOON
(*Dismissing it.*)
See you didn't lose any weight.

DOX
Mashed potatoes, regular hours and exercise. Healthier than I've been since high school.

(*Pause. This has just been chatter to cover their excitement. They are so pleased to see each other there are no words to express their pleasure.*)

SPOON
Damn, jug blower—

DOX
(*Moves away, looking around.*)

SPOON
Three years.

DOX
And ten months. They count too. Three years and ten months of iron, stone and solo sleeping.

(*Still surveying.*)
It's changed, man.

(*Indicating the television & looks accusingly at SPOON.*)

SPOON
    (Shrugs, apologetic)
For ball games—

    (Behind bar. "What you going to have?")

DOX
Ginger ale, on the rocks for me, bartender.

SPOON
For over twenty years I been trying to tell you I ain't a bartender, I'm an inn keeper, and a music impresario.

    (Pours a ginger ale.)

DOX
Well, innkeeper, ginger ale's what I'm drinking. Hear me?

SPOON
    (Pours another ginger ale for himself.)

DOX
Look, Spoon, you don't have to do that, man. I can stand to watch somebody else drink alcohol. I . . .

SPOON
    ("This ain't because of you.")
These days my recreation is thinking of ways to keep from giving my money to Uncle Sam. Death wasn't certain, but taxes are.

DOX
    (Referring to the ginger ale.)
And if I ask you for anything else, I know you got better sense than to give it to me.

SPOON
I just hope you got better sense than to ask.

DOX
You ever know me to do anything in my best interest?

SPOON
You married Lily.

(Toasting gesture at the insight of this last remark, and the action which prompted it. They drink.)

SPOON
You talk to Theresa yet?

DOX
You were supposed to give her the message for me.

SPOON
She'll be here. She wants to see you.

DOX
She tell you that?

SPOON
She'll be here. She's going to have some news for you when she see you.

DOX
I'm hip.

SPOON
Hip to what?

DOX
You just like a woman, you can't keep nothing.

SPOON
What? I didn't say nothing.

DOX
It's a wonder Paulette didn't catch you a long time ago with your big mouth.

SPOON
You don't know what you talking about, I didn't say nothing.

DOX
You would've if I'd given you time.

SPOON
So what you think you know?

DOX
Theresa got an offer to go on the road with Ronnie Nichols.

SPOON
("That's it, all right.")
Right out of the blue he called and asked her.

DOX
(Without enthusiasm.)
I'm hip.

SPOON
(Noting his reaction.)

How'd you hear about it already? She just got the offer day before yesterday herself.

DOX
It's a small world.

(*Changing subject.*)
How's Paulette? I know she's all right—

SPOON
(*Going along with it.*)
You know her. I've never stopped being amazed or amused by Paulette.

DOX
(*With a knowing sadness.*)
The Park sisters. Lily and Paulette.

SPOON
How'd we get so lucky?

DOX
How about Lester and Ben?

SPOON
Who? My sons, the two Sambos? Don't say nothing to me about them two Negroes.

DOX
(*Amused.*)
The two Sambos? Why you call them that, Spoon?

SPOON
Because all them spooks are good for is eating flap jacks and running around in circles.

DOX
(Laughs. His mind elsewhere.)

SPOON
With them two, school's not a stepping stone, like it would have been for us, its an excuse.

DOX
Like Satchmo said, "Don't need a diploma do what we do."

SPOON
But it wouldn't've hurt neither one of us.

DOX
("You're right.")

SPOON
("But you hear what I'm saying.")
Both still at home, scratching and napping. Paulette wants them out of there as much as I do, but she won't say nothing —and won't let me.

DOX
They probably just like everybody else their age: young, hard-headed and confused.

SPOON
I'm the one confused; coming in here six days a week. They got it figured out.

DOX
You could have told me this in-a-letter. Damn near four years and you still got your first time to write.

SPOON
Write you? Whole time I was in the army I didn't even write my mama.

DOX
Not even on Mother's Day?

SPOON
All right, next Mother's Day a card is yours. And I didn't need to hear from you, because I knew what you was doing.

DOX
   (Playing straight man.)
What?

SPOON
Breaking up them f'ing rocks, like in them prison pictures.

DOX
How you know I wasn't skilled labor?

SPOON
You might've made license plates on days it rained. But they had you on rock and road detail the rest of that time, buddy. You ain't jiving me.

DOX
I ought to knock you down and roll you out in traffic.

SPOON
I thought that was what had happened when I had my heart attack.

DOX
I didn't believe Paulette's letter telling that.

SPOON
Believe it.

DOX
That's what you get for being old.

SPOON
That's what I get for living like I was living—and for doing what I was doing when I had it.

DOX
Letter just said you'd had one. What were you doing you shouldn' t' ve been?

SPOON
Playing patty-cake with a twenty-one-year-old, got a body like the Clark Street Cadillac factory, buddy.

DOX
You don't have no better sense than fooling with them young girls, you deserve whatever happened to you.

SPOON
They got a way of renewing your faith in yourself, like a shoeshine or filling an inside straight. But that young girl cured me of a bunch of bad habits. I quit drinking, cussing, smoking, eating fried foods and chasing tail. On-the-spot!, what I'm talking about.

DOX
Hell, you might as well went on and died. Cause giving up all that, you don't have no reason to live no-way.

SPOON
You let your heart attack you and see what you give up, and how soon.

DOX
Who was she?

SPOON
Girl Ben knows from journalism class. Assignment was to do an article about colored business men.

DOX
You dirty old dog.

SPOON
You ain't *seen* her, Dox.

DOX
I bet Paulette hired her to knock you off . . .

SPOON
      ("Why didn't I think of that?")
For my insurance money.

DOX
. . . or as revenge for marrying her in the first place.

SPOON
Paulette know I'm the best thing ever happened to her. Ain't worked a day since we married. But you saying you think this little girl was the bait in a plot on my life?

DOX
What better trap could they laid for you?

SPOON
If she was a hit woman, she was a professional. You hear what I'm saying?

DOX
I hear you.

SPOON
She didn't *never* get tired!

DOX
She wasn't but twenty-one.

SPOON
I figured what was happening was when I'd doze off, one would slip out and they'd run a duplicate in on me.

(Bragging.)
But I'd always see a smile before I did doze.

DOX
My man. —Till your heart attacked you.

SPOON
You don't never want that to happen to you, no matter how good what leads up to it is.

DOX
There are those who would say it serves you right.

SPOON
But you wouldn't be one of them. Would you?

DOX
Not me, not me. Cause I'm your buddy.

SPOON
And the reason we stayed buddies all these years is we ain't made a habit of telling each other what was good for us.

DOX
Solid.

SPOON
Still, I have sworn off fried foods, cigarettes, alcohol and playing the jockey to twenty-one year old stallions.

DOX
And the cussing?

SPOON
Just threw that one in as a bribe, show to God I wasn't bullshitting.

DOX
What did Paulette say when she found out — the particulars.

SPOON
She don't know. Cynthia, that was the girl's name, was hip enough to call an ambulance, and then get a-hold of Benjamin, who, of course, was at home, not having no job to go to. Paulette was out shopping, which didn't surprise nobody. All she does is go shopping and get ready to go shopping. Ben met me at the hospital. Told his mother I'd been at the bar moving liquor cases when it happened.

DOX
So he covered for you.

SPOON
Probably so he can blackmail me so I won't be able to put no pressure on him to vacate.

DOX
And you say they won't work, Spoon? Ben or Lester.

SPOON
God won't live long enough to see the Sambos get a job.

DOX
But, at least you learned a lesson, you say?

SPOON
If nobody ain't never learned from their mistakes I did.

DOX
What would you do if Cynthia—the young stallion, with the stamina of an army mule—was to walk in here right now?

SPOON
And what?

DOX
Tell you she wanted to give you some.

SPOON
(Without consideration.)
I'd be a dead motherfucker by dinner time.

(They laugh.)
You been out for two weeks. I know it didn't take you that long to find your way back home.

DOX
Looked around a little bit. —Did Theresa talk to you? About Nichols' offer. What you thought?

SPOON
She's pretty independent. But we talked about it a little bit.

DOX
And?

SPOON
I told her I thought it was a good chance for her.

DOX
And?

SPOON
I don't know. Ask her.

DOX
If she bothers to come I will.

SPOON
I'll bet this bar against a donut she'll be here.

DOX
Did you tell her what I wanted?

SPOON
    ("Of course.")
You asked me to, didn't you?

DOX
And?

SPOON
> ("And nothing...")

I told her—

DOX
She say anything?

SPOON
> ("I told you.")

Nothing. I told her, "Your daddy says he's coming and..."

DOX
"...and he wants to play some music with you." Did you tell her that?

SPOON
> ("I told her.")

DOX
And what did she say?

SPOON
Nothing.

DOX
How'd she say it? Did she think about it and—frown, or smile, or—How'd she look?

SPOON
Next time send your message by Western Union, maybe they're face-reading experts.

DOX
I sure as hell won't send it by your Al Hibbler ass.

SPOON
What you want me to tell you is something you're going to have to find out for yourself. You tell her, you watch. Then you'll know.

DOX
("Thanks a lot.")

SPOON
She's your daughter. All you're . . .

DOX
I'll see her.

SPOON
(Changing the subject.)
Paulette is expecting you for dinner.

DOX
Theresa must have done *something*. To clue you to what she was thinking.

SPOON
Look! She didn't jump up and down and she didn't break down and cry.

DOX
Damn. All I asked you to do. . .

SPOON
(Hard.)
And I did it. Passing on messages ain't my job.

(Instant tension.)

DOX
(With edge.)
You saying I asked you to do too much already?

SPOON
I did my f'ing job.

DOX
And you saying I didn't do mine?

SPOON
We ain't even talking about that. We talking about...

DOX
I thought that's what *you* was talking about. About how you took over when I fucked up.

SPOON
I just did what was necessary.

DOX
More. You didn't have to and you did. So, now I said it, all right?

SPOON
Naw. I didn't say it for all that.

DOX
But you said it.

SPOON
What I meant was ...

DOX
And as far as I'm concerned it was understood. Y'know.

SPOON
I was. But, see, you getting all . . .

DOX
I ain't getting all nothing. I'm just trying to let you know I know what you did. For Theresa.

SPOON
You ain't got to. . .

    (". . .go through all that.")

DOX
And for me. . .

SPOON
You wrong. . .

DOX
How I'm wrong?

SPOON
We go back too f'ing far. . .

    ("To be going through all this.")

DOX
    (Calming down.)
You right. On them rare occasions when you right, you right.

SPOON
Okay, then—

DOX
Yeah.

SPOON
So, I'm just saying I know you back. And you going to deal with her. All right?

DOX
("I appreciate it.")
(Give each other a light five.)

DOX
(As much to himself as to SPOON.)
She's practically grown now, Spoon. Haven't seen or heard from her in four years. Since she was sixteen.

SPOON
("Yeah, I guess you're right.")

DOX
("So, tell me something.")

SPOON
(Considering it.)
She ain't her mama.

DOX
(Resigned.)
Can't hold that against her. They didn't make but one Lily.

SPOON
(Being careful, wanting to get it right.)
She's—restless. Can be hard headed.

DOX
Like about her getting married.

SPOON
And she can be a bitch, when she makes up her mind to.

DOX
    (Unsure.)
When she wants her way?

SPOON
    ("No, that's not quite it." Clarification rather than alibi.)
She hasn't been coming around too much lately. But—like she's got a chip on her shoulder.

DOX
T 'ward you?

SPOON
Naw, we're pretty cool, y'know.

DOX
T 'ward me?

SPOON
More—just generally, I think—

DOX
Like a singer? That kind of being a bitch?

SPOON
    (Glad for an apt analogy.)
Yeah. Like that. Like a singer.

DOX
      ("Damn. I was afraid of that.")
Singers can be a bitch.

SPOON
Bad as bunions in new shoes.

DOX
Lady Day can be like that.

SPOON
Dinah *is* like that.

DOX
They call Sarah Vaughn *sassy* to keep from calling her something worse.

SPOON
It ain't easy for chicks, singers or musicians.

DOX
Nobody makes them do it.

SPOON
Nobody makes any of us.

DOX
      ("That's a good point. It was a stupid thing for me to say.")
Yeah, you're right. when you're right you're right. Yeah.

SPOON
You're back, you talk to Theresa. Make your own judgments.

DOX
I should've had sense enough to have sons, like you.

SPOON
Knuckleheads— Girls might be easier. You talk to them they might listen.

DOX
Did Theresa listen before she got married?

SPOON
Dox, if it hadn't been so pitiful it would have been funny. But wasn't nothing nobody could tell her. The Sambos even suggested we put out a contract on him. I should have listened to them on that one.

DOX
(Laughs.)
I think that was the first time I was glad I was in jail.

SPOON
But the more we talked against him the more in love with that hophead she'd get.

(Direct. An apology.)
Wasn't nothing or nobody could stop her.

DOX
("I'm hip.")

SPOON
(Laughs.)
I might not've even gone if Theresa hadn't asked me to give her away—

(Pause.)

39

What could I do, Dox? She asked me.

DOX
("It's cool.")
Did you ever figure out why?

SPOON
Maybe to get out on her own— Maybe she's just attracted to—dead beats.

("I still haven't figured it out.")
But I know 3 months was all she could take of him.

DOX
What does Paulette say?

SPOON
That it doesn't come from her side of the family.

DOX
If Theresa had been an orphan, or grew up in the streets I could dig it. If she'd come from somewhere like this kid I met in the joint. He didn't know *nothing*, Spoon. Nothing!

SPOON
Did he even know that?

DOX
What? That he didn't know nothing? *No.*

SPOON
Not even a clue.

DOX

Hadn't been *taught* nothing. In for armed robbery. I'm surprised he knew which end of the gun to point. I don't mean ignorant, but—unschooled.

SPOON

Nobody ever took time to *teach* him.

DOX

Theresa had grown up like that... He didn't even know to brush his teeth every damn day. I knew if I *didn't* show him something, the simplest thing, that when he got out he'd be back inside, inside a month.

SPOON

Inside or dead. So you showed him...

DOX

How to get a sound out of the horn.

("That's all it was.")

SPOON

And once you *showed* him.

DOX

And he *knew* that he *didn't* know...

SPOON

But showed him gentle enough so he wasn't *ashamed* of *not* knowing...

DOX

And didn't have to be *afraid* of *wanting* to know...

SPOON

The Detroit way: like we used to do it: he could learn. If

he wanted to. You would *teach* him.

DOX
The Detroit way.

SPOON
Un huh.

DOX
   ("He blossomed. Blossomed!")
You could see him opening up. Like a flower to the sun.

SPOON
   ("Of course.")
The Detroit way.

DOX
Once I got him to *admit* he wanted to learn the horn.

SPOON
You could *teach* him something then. . .

DOX
Liked- to-worried-me-to-death after that.

SPOON
Just that he knew he didn't know.

DOX
He was willing to learn.

SPOON
That's all you need to know if you want to know.

DOX
Wanted to know everything. And *I* learned teaching him.

SPOON
          ("Of course you did.")
The-Detroit-way. Know that made you feel good.

DOX
That's the way we learned.

SPOON
The way we were *taught*.

DOX
Long way to go, long time to spend, for a simple lesson.

SPOON
Those be the ones sometimes. —How'd you spend the rest of your time?

DOX
Couldn't've made it if I'd been younger.

SPOON
That kid's age.

DOX
But I set up a little music department. Not too much hassle. Practiced everyday.

SPOON
Anybody to blow with?

DOX
Couple of cats, but it was mostly tax dodgers and they didn't have a whole lot of soul. You really think Theresa'll be in?

SPOON
She'll be here. Royst, too. I told him you were coming.

DOX
The TV star... I could not believe it when I heard...

SPOON
Channel 7 every Saturday morning. The kids dig him. Uncle Rooster. And his Rooster Boosters.

DOX
God bless America.

SPOON
Land of opportunity.

DOX
For the opportunists. —Don't seem like that long ago Royst used to come in begging to sit in.

DOX
Bringing dope trying to bribe his way into sessions. But the son of a bitch could handle that trumpet.

SPOON
And not just for a white boy.

DOX
Speaking of somebody could handle something—you remember Valarie Simms?

SPOON
She's still around.

DOX
How's she doing?

SPOON
Fine. You know she married Floyd Tandy.

DOX
Floyd Tandy! I hated that conventional, play-it-safe son of a bitch. Like he had constipation of the soul. Believed everything the newspaper told him. Dressed like he hoped whitefolks were going to invite him to dinner. *Floyd Tandy.*

SPOON
Died. About—a year ago now.

DOX
      (Sarcastic.)
Aw, that's too bad.

SPOON
Left Valarie *well* off. She got 3 or 4 apartment buildings, stocks and stuff. Yeah, she doing real good.

DOX
You know Floyd was all the time trying to hit on Lily.

SPOON
Always trying to *buy* women. . .

DOX
Hate it when a cat can't do nothing but come out of his

pocket...

SPOON
Make it hard on the rest of us.

DOX
Valarie's skin was so smooth, look like it would bust if you touched her. And she could do it, too, you hear me.

SPOON
What made you think of Valarie?

DOX
Man, sitting in that joint you think about everything and everybody.

SPOON
I guess. Asks about you all the time; ought to call her.

DOX
Valarie was like a monkey with a peanut.

SPOON
Yes, *sir*.

DOX
When did you and Valarie...?

SPOON
I—you know, I don't ever remember—

DOX
Since I was gone?

SPOON
Naw, in the old days.

DOX
You lying—

SPOON
Who didn't?

DOX
When?!

SPOON
You want the day and time?

DOX
I want the truth. And the truth is you can't remember 'cause you didn't never.

SPOON
If I didn't nobody did.

DOX
Boy, you ought to be ashamed of yourself, lying like that.

SPOON
You must've forgot who you talking to.

DOX
  ("I still think you lying.")
Bet you one day some scholar going to write a book on the big part getting a nut's played in the history of jazz.

SPOON
Don't leave out business.

DOX
The world. *We* already done the research.

SPOON
Could get Cynthia to help us with the writing. Remind me to show you the paper she did on me.

DOX
I used to sit up in the joint and try to remember every piece I ever had. But you know what? I think I remember the music better.

SPOON
The night I remember best is when you cut Bird to pieces.

DOX
   (Continuing, in a reflective mood.)
More than the women, the high, the money, any of it—the music.

   (Pause. They consider it.)

SPOON
And you don't believe I was with Valarie.

DOX
I believe you think you was, but I don't believe you was. And I'll tell you why I wanted Valarie in the first place.

SPOON
   ("That's obvious.")
Because she was fine.

DOX
On top of that. I knew, almost for a fact, she and Sugar Ray had been fooling around.

SPOON
Sugar Ray Robinson?

DOX
Baddest boxer...

SPOON
...pound for pound...

DOX
...ever knock a white man down.

SPOON
Don't forget Joe now.

DOX
Oh, the Bomber was mean; but pound for pound and pretty with it.

SPOON
 ("*Okay.*")
You didn't say "pretty."

DOX
That was understood.

SPOON
And you say Valarie and Sugar Ray...?

DOX
That's right.

SPOON
And you knew this?

DOX
I wasn't *there*.

SPOON
Go on with it.

DOX
Now I know there ain't no way in the world, I'm going to be able to challenge Sugar. Not in the ring.

SPOON
You'd be dead as me I fool with Cynthia again. . .

DOX
But the squared circle. . .

SPOON
. . .except you wouldn't have none of the fun.

DOX
. . .ain't the only place you can prove yourself.

SPOON
I hear what you're saying.

DOX
Man to man.

SPOON
So to speak.

DOX
So I have to find another—criterion.

SPOON
You're two professionals. So you have to find some—common ground, so to speak. To equal out the challenge.

DOX
Sugar can dance a little, but on the bandstand...

("I'd kill him.")

SPOON
That's your office; where you conduct your business. Even with cats who can play you can draw a line and dare them to cross it. You out blew *Bird* one night.

DOX
("On the other hand...")
I can fight a little...

DOX
If you *have* to.

SPOON
But it's all she wrote, I try to conduct business in *his* office, what you saying.

DOX
So Valarie...

SPOON
Can be like...

DOX
...the *judge,* kind of...

SPOON
...of something you *and* him can do.

DOX
That's right.

SPOON
So! You and Valarie...

DOX
We go toe to toe. —For the full fifteen.

SPOON
So, did you ask her about the Sugar man?

DOX
(*Put-on boastful.*)
His name never came up. —But she did call me Champ.

SPOON
(*Giving five.*)
You know you bad when you match a professional from another arena.

DOX
Thank you.

SPOON
(*"To prove my point."*)
You know how I got possession of this joint?

DOX
(Considers it. Surprised that he doesn't know.)
No.

(A confession.)
Actually I wasn't that sure you really owned it. I always assumed you were fronting for some white man. Like all the rest of the spooks who were so-called owners.

SPOON
Well, at first I was. I was. You were right. Who owned it before me was the gangsters.

DOX
Like Purple Gang gangsters? Them kind of gangsters?

SPOON
("Correct." Makes a finger/thumb pistol, aims at DOX and fires.)

DOX
Well, that's what I figured. Without actually knowing *who*.

SPOON
What he would do is get a bar in a neighborhood that was changing from white to colored...

DOX
Now who was this?

SPOON
("I'll get to that.")
Get a joint, take out a lot of insurance on it, and then eventually burn it down once "we" had taken over the neighborhood, see. See, this wasn't the first place I'd managed for this guy. He liked me, because I was hip to

all the various little tricks the bartenders and waitresses used to skim off money: false pockets, double receipts, all that, and I kept them honest.

DOX
(Knowing better.)
And you wasn't skimming nothing, huh?

SPOON
("I was, but...")
I had a family to support—

(Laughs.)
And I was slick enough to look honest. Anyway, I fell in love with this joint the first time I ever set foot in it. Wished it was mine from day one.

DOX
Okay.

SPOON
You know my daddy got run out the South.

DOX
("I'm hip.")
For not letting them crackers ride him like a mule.

SPOON
And the thing that hurt him till the day he died, was he wasn't going to be able to pass a plot of land on to me, like his father done for him. "Own some land," that was his song.

DOX
(With subtext.)

My daddy had a different song.

SPOON
Up here it seemed to me like "land" translated into "business." You see what I'm saying.

DOX
I hear you.

SPOON
A business was what I wanted to pass on to my sons. But there was no way, on what I was making *and* stealing, I could afford to buy it. So, in the mean time I'm running it for this guy: and at the end of every week I'd deliver the bag with all the profits to him. In cash, see.

DOX
Northern share-cropping.

SPOON
Then, after a year or so, three or four weeks go by, and I don't hear from him. Nothing. Then I get a call and he tells me not to leave nothing in the joint that night I might want the next day.

DOX
Uh oh, I smell smoke.

SPOON
("*Exactly.*")
The minute the match is struck I'm out of work.

DOX
But you knew it was coming...

SPOON
Sooner or later... But hearing him say it, look like it almost give me my first heart attack.

DOX
Getting an honest, nine to five J-O-B ever cross your mind?

SPOON
(Quickly and finally.)
Going to "swing and sway with Sammy Kaye ever cross yours?"

DOX
Enough said.

SPOON
It wasn't just the job, it was the place too. I was in love with it. See, I knew all along this joint was just a little side operation for this guy. A personal thing aside from his real, big time, gangster business.

DOX
It's your livelihood, but it ain't nothing but a hobby for him.

SPOON
Mainly so he can be around the strippers, you dig.

DOX
Pocket change.

SPOON
That's right. So, that night, I meet him, with the sack from the safe. Something ain't right. Something else was

happening, I can feel it. First of all, he-is-double scared. I know, being who he is he is not *that* scared of the law, local or federal. In fact, he wasn't the kind of scared you be about money, or doing time— He was scared for his life kind of scared. And I figure it must be his own people that he is that scared of.

And for a few minutes we just sit there, like two old maids in church. Nobody saying nothing. Finally I says, real cool, I'm playing it like I'm George Raft, see. I says, "How you doing?"

DOX
Edward G. Robinson is my man.

SPOON
George Raft: "How you doing?," you know, and he says, confidential: the whole nature of his business is about to change in a *big* way, and he's got to lay low till he can make it happen. We sit some more...

DOX
Two old maids.

SPOON
Till I finally say, "If there's anything I can do—", just like that, y'know, George Raft.

DOX
Cool. It's what you say anyway, to somebody with a problem.

SPOON
And he like looked at me like I was Santa Claus and he's three-years-old.

DOX
All because you just said—

SPOON
"If there's anything I can do. . ." For a minute I thought, "This white man's going to kiss me." He says he doesn't know why he didn't think of me in the first place; says he knows he can trust me; and right then I was just about the only person he knew who he could trust.

DOX
You knew then it was his own people was after him.

SPOON
 ("*Exactly.*")
Said he needed a big favor. And he'd pay me what-ever I asked.

DOX
The boy was serious.

SPOON
As suicide. It was one of those moments, Dox. A classic. I started to say the money that I already had in the sack.

DOX
But he hadn't mentioned the money. . .

SPOON
 (*Pantomimes clandestinely pushing the money sack out of sight.*)

DOX
So you don't. Maybe he's so scared he'll forget it.

SPOON
Then I thought I'll ask him for some *different* money. Enough to put the Sambos through school (there was enough for that in the sack), and maybe a vacation or fur coat for Paulette. A chance to do something for them, y'know.

DOX
He asked *you*, so wasn't no time for being shy.

SPOON
Whatever it is it's got something to do with his life.

DOX
So maybe he ain't in no mood to negotiate.

SPOON
That's what I'm thinking. And too, I thought about my daddy, and the Sambos, and how this guy was making money off us on both ends.

DOX
While he's in business and afterwards, too. And we end up with the ashes.

(With admiration.)
And you thought all this in that minute.

SPOON
That *second*.

DOX
(Giving five.)
They don't teach that at Miller Junior High.

SPOON
      ("Exactly.")
And without skipping a beat, I said I'd do what-ever it was, sight unseen. . .

DOX
Uh huh?

SPOON
For the papers on this joint. And his promise not to burn it.

DOX
The element of surprise. He was expecting you to ask for money. Because they think that's all we're interested in.

SPOON
And I crossed him up.

DOX
Shifted on his ass, and made him play *your* game.

SPOON
As soon as I said it I knew I had him.

DOX
Like with a lady, the first time.

SPOON
      ("Right.")
You can *feel* it.

DOX
You *know*.

SPOON
Wham—

(Holding out his hand for five, as:)

DOX

(Gives him five.)

Bam!

SPOON
Thank you ma'am! —Dox, he didn't even blink.

DOX
You had him! So what you have to do?

SPOON
Go to the airport, get a suitcase and tickets from a locker. Take the plane to Mexico. Switch suitcases with a big heavy ass one in a locker down there, come back home. Put *it* in a locker.

DOX
I thought you was going to have to bump off the emperor or whatever they got down there.

SPOON
(Shakes his head.)

DOX
But you would have done it.

SPOON
(Firing thumb & forefinger "gun.")
Hasta luego, El Presidente.

DOX
So?

SPOON
So, just that slick, the deed, putting the joint in my name, was here, waiting on me when I got back!

DOX
Wham bam. But I still don't know who it was.

SPOON
        ("Wait a minute.")
The very next morning after I get back, I'm congratulating myself and having my coffee, it comes on the news: Terrible Tony...

DOX
Terrible Tony? You telling me it was The Terrible Tony?

SPOON
        ("That's who.")
Mmm hmmm—

DOX
He was the biggest, *baddest,* most notorious... He was to Detroit what Al Capone— One slip with him...

SPOON
And Paulette got to cancel a day of shopping to go to my funeral.

DOX
Bang, bang, shoot 'em up. I remember when he got killed.

SPOON
Found floating under the Belle Isle bridge.

DOX
They say so many holes in him looked like granny's lace curtains.

SPOON
That's what came on the news. It was the morning after I'd made the delivery.

DOX
Man. You and Terrible Tony.

SPOON
But now all kinds of questions are running through my mind. Who got him? Why? It got anything to do with whatever it was I just delivered?

DOX
'Cause if they'll shoot him you can imagine what they'll do to you.

SPOON
    ("Exactly!")
And what about Paulette and the boys?, you know.

DOX
Spoon, you took a hellified chance dealing with him, toe to toe like that. I'm proud to know you, boy.

SPOON
It was worth it, for Paulette and them.

DOX
    (Serious.)
I didn't do that good by Theresa. And she knows it.

SPOON
If I'd know then how the Sambos was going to turn out, I probably wouldn't've done none of it.

> *(We hear corny, "Howdy Doody" type theme as ROYST enters with a burst of energy. He is already on his way to being intoxicated. Does few steps of Rooster Walk before he sees DOX)*

Cockle doodle doo!

Dox!

DOX
Royst! My man.

> *(They greet each other, trading scatted fours on Groovin' High.)*

SPOON
He doesn't come around much since he got to be a big television star. Do you? This man here have to escape from the big house to get you in here.

ROYST
You'd think because I'm a television star I could get some kind of respect. And a drink. But he's lying as usual. I'm here at least twice a month.

SPOON
I'd starve to death all my customers was on that schedule.

ROYST
Don't I make up in volume what I lack in consistency?

SPOON
> *(Pouring drink.)*

You got a point, my man.

ROYST
(To *DOX.*)
So, tell me about...

DOX
No. You tell me, *Uncle Rooster.*

ROYST
(*To* SPOON)
Did you tell him the story?

DOX
You tell me.

ROYST
Little Bobby Boyd, you remember him.

DOX
Burlesque comic, big ass checkerboard suit, works strip joints, the Gaiety, the National...

ROYST
Used to. He gets lucky, lands a gig as Uncle Bobby on Channel 7. On every Saturday morning, showing cartoons, eating breakfast with the kiddies.

DOX
I wouldn't let him near my kids—

SPOON
Dig this. How a cat can have the golden goose and...

ROYST
He's cooled out. Dig. I'm playing in the little group he's got on the show. Tom Samanski, piano, Davie Throraux,

65

bass, Charlie Viola drums, and me. We do little bits, nothing much. A dream gig, dig.

DOX
You always liked clowning with the audience.

ROYST
A natural talent. Secret to this gig is not to go to bed from Friday night.

SPOON
Anyway...

ROYST
This stripper, Tawny The Torch; Bobby's swinging with her. In love like he invented it! But he finds she's going to split to Toledo to set up house keeping with her drummer.

DOX
Ow!

ROYST
And it breaks his heart.

DOX
Didn't know burlesque comics had hearts.

SPOON
First I heard of it.

ROYST
Everybody has one. And Bobby's is broken. Goes on a three day drunk, Wednesday, Thursday, Friday. Saturday morning he wobbles in to the show, last minute. Plowed.

Goes on. This little girl, innocent, you know—like the little chick in Frankenstein.

>(LITTLE GIRL.)
"Uncle Bobby, Uncle Bobby! Give my dolly a kiss." — Bobby goes berserk!

DOX
On the air?

ROYST
Live television, man! Screaming at this little chick she's going to grow up just like all the rest of the no good painted and perfumed women God made, end up like a taunting Jezebel or whore of Babylon, and run off with a drummer, don't know a rim shot from his asshole. Yaba daba da! Then to cap it off Bobby pukes all over Little Miss Moppet, and her dolly. Live! Well I step in and save the day. And, long story short I am offered the gig.

DOX
As *Uncle Rooster*.

ROYST
>*("And the rest is show business history." Sudden thought.)*

Oh, wait man, seriously, I was so excited about seeing you. Did you hear?

>*(Presenting glass for another drink.)*

DOX
What?

ROYST
Spoon?

SPOON
      (Pouring)
What's that, Royst?

ROYST
I was sure you would have. By now.

DOX
      (Off-handed)
Tell me or shut up about it—

ROYST
Bird is dead, man.

      (Shock and instant tension. Music.)

SPOON
Bird?

DOX
Dead?

      (Pause. He almost asks for a drink. Stops himself. Downs the ginger ale in a gulp. Moves away from the bar stunned.

      Music stops.)

ROYST
The 12th.

DOX
Two days ago?

SPOON
Naw, see that can't be. We would have heard something.

ROYST
I'm telling you.

DOX
Maybe you heard it wrong.

SPOON
He was just in here. What? This is — March. Last month.

ROYST
I'm hip.

DOX
Maybe it was somebody else.

ROYST
No.

SPOON
Standing right there where you standing.

DOX
Maybe it just sounded...

ROYST
Give me some credit, man.

SPOON
(To *DOX)*
The middle of f'ing February.

ROYST
Last month.

SPOON
He was...

ROYST
At the Rouge,

(*To* DOX)
the Rouge Lounge.

DOX
I know about the Rouge!

SPOON
Naw, naw. Supposed to be, to double with Johnny Smith, but, naw, it didn't never happen.

ROYST
The Rouge.

SPOON
Don't tell me.

ROYST
I thought...

SPOON
Like lit. At the Madison. Doing a single.

ROYST
The Madison?

SPOON
With Candy-Johnson's-band. Boo Boo Turner, Benny Benjamin... At-the-Madison.

ROYST
Maybe—

SPOON
I know it. Came in. Didn't have overcoat the first. Nothing but a blue suit. Gave him a rum and Coke. "Man, you better get you some more clothes, Bird." "I'm thinking about flying south from here, Spoon, so it don't matter." That's what he said. Standing right there. No horn, no overcoat.

ROYST
    (The alcohol's effect becoming more evident.)
Yeah, Spoon, man, you're right.

SPOON
I know it.

    (To DOX.*)*
Asked about you.

DOX
Did?

ROYST
I was here, I remember.

SPOON
    (To DOX*)*
We laughed about the night you out blew him.

DOX
Yeah.

SPOON
        (To ROYST*)*
Where'd you hear this?

ROYST
Mort called me from the Apple. Says Bird was up at the Baroness' place, died up there.

SPOON
What from?

ROYST
A bunch of shit, you know. And the word was slow getting out because, I guess, I don't know, because supposedly nobody claimed the body, for some reason.

DOX
You say he was at the Baronesses' place, right? Then she would have seen to somebody claiming the body.

SPOON
Yeah, it don't make sense. Mort must have got it wrong.

ROYST
I'm telling you, man—

SPOON
        (To DOX.*)*
Does that sound right to you?

DOX
Naw, not to me neither—

ROYST
I asked him the same questions you're asking me, but he

swore it was true. —I'm sorry I had to be the one to tell you. But I thought...

DOX
I was on a train all night. Didn't even pick up a paper...

SPOON
Ben or Lester always get the morning *Free Press* before me—I guess we knew it was coming.

DOX
Bird. Damn!

SPOON
When did you say it was, exactly?

ROYST
The 12th. March the 12th.

DOX
Two days ago.

SPOON
Saturday night.

ROYST
It must have been around 9 o'clock because they say he was watching the Dorsey Show.

SPOON
I had that on. The Dorsey Show. We were watching that in here. The cats didn't start blowing until after 10. Man. You say Bird was watching that too, huh?

ROYST
That's what Mort said.

SPOON
"I'm flying south from here," that's what he said.

DOX
Two things I'll always remember: the first time I saw Lily, and the first time I heard Bird.

> *(Pause.)*

SPOON
I remember when I first heard that Roosevelt was dead.

ROYST
But he was, what, an old man, you know. Not that you expected it, but still—

SPOON
But you know what I mean.

> *(Pause. Laughs. Brighter.)*

Still, Bird got the most out of it while he was here.

DOX
> *(Laughs knowingly.)*

SPOON
Deed he did. I used to get mad enough at him to kill him.

DOX
But you had to love him.

SPOON
Had to. The first time he ever played in here they took a

break at the end of the first set. Naturally, it was Sardine City. But I didn't mind the long breaks he took, because people drank when Bird was around. But this one night...

DOX
I know what you talking about, I remember.

SPOON
Yeah, that's right, you were playing that night.

ROYST
I was here...

SPOON
People are pissed because they were slow getting served. Come to find out one of my waitresses is missing.

DOX
           (*To* ROYST.)
Chick's name was Thomasina. Lived on Cardoni.

ROYST
You know I remember Thommie.

SPOON
Soon as I realized she was missing I *knew* what was happening!

ROYST
Why wouldn't I remember her?

SPOON
And sent somebody over to her house with a message: she wasn't in here in five minutes serving drinks she was fired for-ever.

ROYST
You cats forget I was always around.

SPOON
And to tell Bird I didn't care who he screwed, *unless* it was taking money out of my pocket.

ROYST
I was here too, you know. It wasn't just you guys.

SPOON
He apologized when he got back. You know how Bird could get all formal and proper:

(*As* Bird.)
"Spoon, you, being a man of the world, like myself, understand how when, in the heat of the moment, the more primitive urges take precedence over merely economic considerations." I never will forget that...

(*They laugh.*)

ROYST
Me either.

DOX
Yeah, he had his fun.

SPOON
I'm telling you, he was just in here not a month ago. It won't be as easy now.

DOX
If all the alto players think they automatically move up a notch because he's gone, they've got another think coming.

(*Music.*)

SPOON
May he rest in peace.

ROYST
—Me, too... Spoon?

(*Music fades.*)

SPOON
Yeah, go ahead. Your cots waiting on you.

ROYST
(*Rising and moving to exit to back.*)
Just for a minute. I'll be good as new. Got a rehearsal in a few... Dox, man, welcome back.

(*He is gone.*)

SPOON
That's how it is now.

(*They drink.*)

SPOON
Know what I realized? The young cats that were coming up when you—left, they've come up, and split for the Apple.

DOX
I ran into some of them when I passed through there.

SPOON
We're the old timers now, Dox.

DOX
—Yeah, Spoon, I'm hip—

SPOON
Know what's crossed my mind a couple of times lately.

DOX
What's that?

SPOON
Selling it to somebody.

DOX
What for?

SPOON
I'm tired of paying taxes, and Ben and Lester ain't interested...

DOX
Hell, that would be like being—beat. It was Christmas Eve in here every night. If you think about it, history was made in here.

SPOON
—Do you realize we just found out Bird is dead?

(Pause.)

DOX
So you say you think Theresa might be in?

SPOON
She'll be here. I'm telling you.

DOX
(Doubtful.)
I shouldn't've told her what I wanted. Gives her too much time to think of ways to say no.

SPOON
Why's yalls playing together so important?

DOX
Because if we do then I'll know: how she's doing—know what she feels.

SPOON
Why we make them so important?

DOX
Looks like everybody else is dying, or giving up—

SPOON
To hell with 'em, the Sambos, Theresa. The future ain't ours to control. You know what we ought to do? Run down to New Orleans, for a week of voodoo poontang and fillet gumbo.

DOX
Think so?

SPOON
I ever lied to you?

THERESA
(*Enters, unnoticed by either of them.*)

DOX
How about Valarie?

SPOON
(*Laughs.*)
All right, *maybe*. *Maybe* I didn't. Maybe I just thought I did.

(They laugh.)

THERESA
Afternoon, Uncle Spoon.

DOX & SPOON
    (Shocked.)
    (Music.)

SPOON
Hey, T, baby.

DOX
Your Uncle Spoon ain't the only one in here.

THERESA
Hello, daddy.

    (Music up.)

END OF ACT ONE

(ACT TWO
As above. No time has passed.)

DOX
(Motions Theresa to a table. She pauses. He moves to it, stands. She joins him. He holds her chair for her. She sits. He returns to the bar to get his glass. Joins her. Showing her his glass.)
Ginger ale.

(Looks to SPOON for affirmation. To THERESA.)
What're you having?

THERESA
(Shaking her head, conceding nothing.)
I didn't come to drink. I...

DOX
(Interrupting, his hand on hers.)
You came to see me, didn't you? And now you're here. Have something.

THERESA
I don't want anything.

DOX
With me.

THERESA
I've got stuff to do.

DOX
We don't get this chance everyday.

    (To SPOON.)
Give her what she usually has.

SPOON
    (Prepares to get a Coke with a little ice.)

THERESA
    (To SPOON. "Don't.")
Uncle Spoon.

DOX
It won't slow you down.

    (To SPOON. "Give it to her.")
We can still do what you came for.

SPOON
    (Delivering the Coke.)
With a little ice.

THERESA
    ("Traitor.")
Thanks.

SPOON
    (Returns to bar.)

DOX
    (Holding his glass for a toast.)
You want to do the honors?

THERESA
    (Silence.)

DOX
May the music live.

>**THERESA**
>>*(Pause as she wavers.)*
>
>**DOX**
>>*(Drinks.)*
>
>**THERESA**
>>*(Sips, a compromise.)*

DOX
So you doing all right—on your own?

>**THERESA**

I do okay—on my own.

>**DOX**

You look good.

>**THERESA**
>>*(Reluctant admission.)*

You too.

>**DOX**

Spoon. Didn't want me facing you in stripes and a number across my chest.

>**THERESA**

You'd probably look good in stripes, too.

>>*(Almost involuntarily brushes at lent, fixes pocket handkerchief or some needless, but very business-like action.)*

How do you feel?

DOX
Good. I feel good.

THERESA
That's good.

DOX
Better than I can remember.

THERESA
How was prison? —That's a stupid question, huh? Did they treat you all right?, I guess I mean.

DOX
The routine was the worse thing.

THERESA
I wondered a lot about it, but I don't have any idea what it's really like.

DOX
No reason you should.

THERESA
("Let's get down to business.")
So, what's the best way to do this?

DOX
Do what?

THERESA
(Wanting to be tough.)
Play father/daughter. See if I'm. . .

DOX
>(*Matching her tone and attitude.*)

—clean behind the ears.

THERESA
>(*Still tough.*)

You think you know me well enough to tell that?

DOX
>(*Tougher.*)

You ain't the first female I've ever met. And most of them had more experience at it than you.

THERESA
>(*Weaker, but trying to tough it out.*)

Oh, so I'm just like all of them?

DOX
>(*Mean.*)

What makes you so much different?

THERESA
>(*Hurt. Weaker.*)

I'm your daughter, for one thing.

DOX
>(*Softer.*)

I knew that before you did. And I haven't forgotten it.

>(*End of round two. Apologetic.*)

I didn't bring you anything.

THERESA
>(*Lighter, as it relieved.*)

That's what you used to do when I was a little girl.

DOX
What makes you think you're still not a little girl?

THERESA
It's not like I was expecting some ashtray shaped like the electric chair.

DOX
I wasn't sure what you—

THERESA
I didn't expect anything.

DOX
I wrote you a long letter.

THERESA
I never got it.

DOX
I never sent it.

THERESA
When did you write it?

DOX
Around the time you got married.

THERESA
Oh—

DOX
>(At a loss.)

Royst is in the back.

THERESA
Crying the blues?

DOX
>(Laugh.)

THERESA
He can afford 'em on what they pay him to do what he does.

DOX
You being kind of hard on him aren't you?

THERESA
Everything's so easy for him. It just irks me he's got the nerve to complain about being left out of the music, that's all.

DOX
That what he does?

THERESA
Must've been too drunk to get into that speech.

SPOON
Or not drunk enough.

DOX
Okay. How about you then? Tell me you've turned into a nice little piano player, huh?

THERESA
      (Pleased, but wanting to hide it.)
Who?

DOX
I asked around.

THERESA
You asked, or they just volunteered it?

DOX
Both. How's your sight reading? Any better?

THERESA
I can sight read fly specks.

DOX
Bird died. Did you hear?

THERESA
Yeah. He was a funny man.

DOX
It's hard to believe. It's going to be different.

THERESA
He hasn't done too much lately.

DOX
      (Strong.)
He did enough for-ever!

THERESA
      (Apologetic.)

I saw on the way over here where somebody wrote on a wall: "Bird Lives."

DOX
Bird lives. . .

THERESA
So, what are you going to do?

DOX
First I was thinking about Europe. See what it's like where people respect musicians.

THERESA
But you're changed your mind?

DOX
I might put a group together. Good young cats with fresh ideas. I can teach them the rest. I heard you had an offer—

THERESA
Uncle Spoon told you.

SPOON
What make you think it was me?

THERESA
Because you're like an old refrigerator. Can't keep nothing.

SPOON
I think I resent that.

THERESA
You can resent it all you want, but the truth is you two haven't kept nothing from each other since Jesus turned water into wine.

SPOON
  (Amused.)
Put you in the mind of Paulette just then, didn't she?

DOX
  (Amused.)
Your sound was as much yours as your sense of humor I wouldn't have nothing to worry about.

THERESA
How do you know about my sound, and what's wrong with it?

DOX
I heard tapes.

THERESA
I suppose you didn't have anything to do with that either.

DOX
He would have if I'd asked him. . .

THERESA
So, what was wrong with the tape?

DOX
I heard a lot of your mama in your playing.

THERESA
    (Defensive.)
I'm her daughter, too.

DOX
But telling *your* story's what's it all about. Otherwise you might as well be slinging steel out to Mr. Ford's foundry.

THERESA
Well, it doesn't matter anyway, does it Uncle Spoon.

DOX
Why doesn't it?

THERESA
Because I'm going to retire from the jazz life.

DOX
    (Shocked, but cool.)
You serious?

THERESA
Oh, he didn't tell you that, huh?

DOX
No he didn't.

THERESA
You didn't ask him?, or too busy talking about important stuff, like women?

DOX
When you decide this?

THERESA
A while ago.

DOX
And you say Spoon knew it?

SPOON
From now on, you got anything to say to each other, do me a favor and just say it. Now I'm going wake Royst up so he can get where he has to go.

THERESA
Stay. You're family. I don't have any secrets from you—

DOX
Just from me, huh?

SPOON
    (Exiting.)
I'm still going to have to eavesdrop. You know I'm going to have to tell Paulette *something*.

    (Exits to rear.)

DOX
So, what?

THERESA
Be something other than some jazz woman.

DOX
You say that like its something wrong with it.

THERESA
I know what you're going to say.

DOX
    ("What?")

THERESA
It was good enough for my mother—

DOX
    (Silent.)

THERESA
You made your choices, Mama made hers. I'm going to make mine.

DOX
You going to go back with what's his name?, give that another try?

THERESA
    ("You know what his name is.")
LeRoy. And no, that's over with.

DOX
Sorry he wasn't around long enough for me to meet him.

THERESA
He said the same thing about you.

DOX
So, how is he?

THERESA
Like you care.

DOX
I do if you do.

THERESA
>*(Trying to end it.)*

Haven't seen him for awhile.

DOX

Well, if he's not worth talking about—

THERESA
>*(Defensive.)*

He needed me.

>*(Laughs. Honest.)*

If he didn't need me, nobody did.

DOX

From what I hear he needed more than you.

THERESA
>*("Yeah.")*

He had more than his share of problems. And, yeah, he stayed bombed all the time. But I dug him *because* getting in his head was like waking up in a room full of mirrors.

He told me one time about all the things be on his mind everyday while he was trying to score. I mean it's not simple at *all*. He was more complicated than 7 or 8 of these college boys. There's all these considerations and decisions—every-day—just to get some dope to get all the dumb daytime stuff off his mind. Always thinking. Plotting. He wasn't just some hophead. —Well he was, but he was deeper than that, than what you'd think a hop head was, see.

DOX

I know all about hopheads.

THERESA
Well, anyway, he needed somebody. I thought I could take an outlaw and cure him.

DOX
Tame him, you mean. With outlaws, you take 'em, or leave 'em, but you don't tame 'em.

THERESA
Where were you with all this good advice when I needed you?

DOX
Maybe you learned more by my not stopping you.

THERESA
That why you're not trying to talk me out of quitting the music?

DOX
You said it: every tub has to sit on its own bottom.

THERESA
That's right. And all I want is to be—

DOX
What?

THERESA
(Tough admission.)
—Ordinary—

DOX
(Laughs.)

THERESA
(Hurt.)
Don't laugh at me like I'm some child.

DOX
You mean ordinary like—Ozzie and Harriet?

THERESA
The straight life, you dig: regular; a husband with a regular job and regular hours and a dog and some kids.

DOX
And where you at in all this?

THERESA
In a family: doing what the average regular chicks are doing: jelly sandwiches for the kids, dinner on time for hubby, shopping, gossiping on the phone—

DOX
I'd seen signs you were going to be ordinary, I'd've tied you in a sack and drowned you while you were still a baby.

("Now let's see if I understand.")
The straight life; and that's why you married this LeRoy, to be ordinary?

THERESA
Shows how little practical guidance I'd had.

DOX
And as for being ordinary, you was a bebop baby, you know that, too?

THERESA
(An accusation.)
I know I'm heading for school in the morning, here come mommy and daddy in from last night's gig. Till I started kindergarten I thought Ben and Lester were the only other kids in the world. And I didn't think we were really kids, just three adults too short to drink or smoke. You know how I learned chemistry? Watching Uncle Spoon mix drinks.

DOX
(Countering.)
And geography from cats talking about gigs on the road. The life is in your blood, baby.

THERESA
Well, I'm going to get it out.

DOX
So, is that it? You blame me because you didn't have an ordinary childhood? And...

THERESA
Who said I blame you for anything.

DOX
Because you didn't have a yard with a picket fence to play in the music's going to lose a piano player.

THERESA
Anyway you said I was just a mimeo of mama.

DOX
But you learning. —Is it the women then?

THERESA
What?

DOX
What our problem is?

THERESA
Whose?

DOX
> (Losing patience.)

Yours and mine.

THERESA
Who said we had a problem?

DOX
> (Exasperated.)

You're like Sugar Ray, you know that.

THERESA
Robinson? How come you say that?

DOX
Anybody tries to come at you straight is in trouble. Wake up in the dressing room, doctor shining a light in your eyes, asking you what city you in, son?

THERESA
I don't know what you're talking about.

DOX
Don't bullshit the bullshitter.

ROYST
    (enters, followed by SPOON.)
Hey, Theresa.

THERESA
    (Not pleased to see him.)
Royst.

ROYST
    (To DOX.)
You know what I'd advise. . .

THERESA
    (Angry. Signifying.)
Advise who?

ROYST
Dox.

THERESA
You? Wearing them rickey-tic white buck shoes; 7 days a week this man out dresses and out plays you. And you advising him?

ROYST
    (Another thought, drunk-serious, to DOX.)
. . .you were my hero, man. You could drink more brandy than any man I've ever met. And it never made him drunk. Did it Spoon?

DOX
    (Impatient)
I thought you were going to give me advice and you writing me a love letter.

ROYST
Wise up, Dox. Get out of it.

(*Pause.*)

That's my advice. You're never going to make any money.

THERESA
(*Not wanting him to be right.*)
He already made some.

DOX
We knew from the jump we weren't going to be millionaires off BeBop.

THERESA
What'd you wake him up for?

ROYST
If Bird couldn't, who could?

SPOON
(*Heard it before.*)
"If he was so great how come he wasn't rich?", huh?

ROYST
I bet I make more in a week...

DOX
It ain't about the money.

ROYST
Kicks, right? Have a blast.

(*"Yeah, I'm hipped to all that."*)
The joy of hanging out, jamming, huh? The Detroit Way.

But it's changing. With most of the young cats it's about charts and ensembles. They can't play without a music stand in front of them.

> (*MUSIC TEACHER a la LAWRENCE WELK.*)

"Today, class, we are going to practice the G 7th chord, remember your posture, and no vibrato, think European, European. All together now... A-one, a-two, a-one, two, three, four..."

> (*Makes fart-like sound.*)

And even if you could find a session,

> (*Directed to* THERESA.)

you have to be asked before you can dance, dig it. "Yeah, we'd love to have you play with us, but you don't know the chart, man."

> (*Himself.*)

And they don't know it but they're losing the people, man. Everything's changing.

THERESA
Yes, *Uncle Rooster*.

ROYST
Uncle Rooster is with kids, man. And I'm telling you, there is no joy. And you can't blame them. What do they know? Korea. Brainwashing. McCarthy. Scandals. The Cold War.

THERESA
Racism.

ROYST
They don't have time for anything complicated as BeBop,

man. They just want to dance.

THERESA
Dance; like you do, back and forth between the music and Uncle Rooster's Barnyard.

ROYST
Uncle Rooster sees what's happening. The bubble is going to bust, with-a-bang. And maybe soon. It's in their eyes, man.

DOX
(With an edge.)
Lighten up, man.

ROYST
She doesn't want to jam with me, man. And none of the cats she hangs with.

THERESA
Nobody likes a gloomy drunk.

ROYST
She's the reason I quit coming around. She was one way when we were alone: "Hey, Roys, man..." But somebody completely different when she was with some of her friends.

DOX
What's he talking about?

ROYST
That's what's really scary. I feel this other, this "whitey" thing; coming like a wall of frigid North Pole wind. Like all of a sudden, to everybody under thirty, everybody

colored and under thirty, all of a sudden I'm white.

> YOUNG BLACK MAN
> Hey, man, you wanna know something, man, you *white*."

THERESA
What do you call it?

ROYST
I mean, like, no shit, man. Like what am I supposed to do about it?

THERESA
Aw, man...

ROYST
I remember when there was no difference.

THERESA
You thought.

ROYST
Not from the musician's point of view. We hung loose, got high together, everything; around the music. Together.

THERESA
You left the music, the music didn't leave you.

ROYST
If there was a problem it was man to man. You. Me. This used to be more like my home than my home.

DOX
It's different for her...

THERESA
You don't have to explain for me.

ROYST
I don't understand. But they're the future. And they're choosing up sides.

THERESA
They were chosen for us.

SPOON
Maybe you have to look at it from their point of view...

ROYST
I don¹t deserve being lumped with some redneck just because my skin's the same color as his—

THERESA
What you want to hear, Royst?

ROYST
Bird is dead, man. A fucking pauper. A goddamn genius. And that's the official end of bebop, man. You watch. White people are going to get control of the music again. Put it back in the hands of amateurs. They're going to find somebody with your sound and my color, and he is going to be crowned on the spot.

(WHITE RECORD EXECUTIVE)
"Start the presses, alert the media. We've found him, George! —Who?! The new King of Music!, that's who. Sounds just like a woogie. But my little girl, Junie Mae, can look at him and I won't have nightmares about Mau Maus—

Naw, he ain't passing, and he ain't a Commie. He's the

genuine article; white as you and me. And as soon as he's declared The New King..."

THERESA
Like Paul White-man, and Benny Good-man...

ROYST
"...that'll wipe that Holier-than-thou attitude off their monkey mugs. Stop them hipsters from strutting around like they got something that we lost. And then we'll have them *exactly* where we fucking A want them, by God!"

(*Himself.*)
It's going to come to that. Three chords, a dump, dump, dump, dump beat. And then you might as well start for the moon, Jim, because our music will be through on this planet.

THERESA
And where'll you be, Royst?

ROYST
Where *I've* always been. Where I was when you were just a baby. I don't want to see that happen to you, Dox. Get out like I did.

THERESA
You going to give him a gig playing barnyard ditties on your show?

ROYST
Bird is dead, man. Another dead duck. Maybe it's for the best. Maybe now everybody can stop thinking he's the only one with a corner on the truth, and couldn't nobody else say nothing.

(Pause.)

All right, he was great. But was he *that* much better than me? And everybody else?

DOX
Yeah.

THERESA
That's how come you quit? So you could do the Rooster Walk?

DOX
You had that choice.

ROYST
You too, huh?

DOX
Me too, what?

ROYST
I feel a North Pole breeze...

DOX
Maybe *you* opened the window.

ROYST
I never had to worry about keeping it closed—before.

DOX
You take the horn out your mouth, you still a white boy. I take it out mine I'm still a spook.

ROYST
Is that *my* fault?

DOX
Is it mine?

THERESA
How 'bout that gig, Royst?

ROYST
I never saw a cat go downhill like you, man. Like a run away train hauling lead bricks. You weren't dependable, no shape to play when you did show. Right, Spoon? Before Lily died you couldn't stand to leave the city, after, you couldn't stand to be in it—

DOX
That you or that sauce talking?

ROYST
Maybe I run my mouth too much—

(Holds up drink as an excuse.)

I just don't get much of a chance to talk music much anymore; cats at the station don't know from nothing about what we're talking about.

SPOON
You know what time it is?

ROYST
Oh, man, thanks for reminding me.

        (To DOX.*)*
I got a rehearsal. Lots of cats on the clock. And a meeting. Talk about maybe going daily. Got to split.

        DOX
Good seeing you.

        ROYST
You going to blow tonight?

        DOX
Maybe. Maybe me and Theresa...

        ROYST
I'll come back. Maybe bring my horn. Sit in. If it's cool, with her, and you— Like we used to. Be cool, huh?

        DOX
Cool.

        ROYST
Anyway, you'll be around. We missed you. Everybody'll be in to hear you.

        DOX
        (Nods.)

        ROYST
Great to have you back, man. Really.

        (Preparing to exit.)
Spoon.

        DOX
Roys.

ROYST
Theresa.

THERESA
(Nods.)

ROYST
I still say they just made an example out of you, because you were colored, *and* a musician.

(A joke.)
It's a wonder you didn't get the chair.

DOX
Thanks for not bringing it up at the time, my man.

ROYST
They're the future, Dox. I don't understand them, I really don't.

SPOON
You're not by yourself.

ROYST
Till next time, Rooster Boosters.

(Does few steps of Rooster Walk.)
Cock a doodle doo!

(Pause. Exits.)
(Music.)

SPOON
He won't be back tonight. Be another couple weeks.

DOX
He's really hurting...

THERESA
Damn some Royst. Damn all the Roysts. Royst get on my nerves anyway. The only reason he got a chance in the music in the first place was you gave it to him. Right? Then, all of a sudden, when things get a little rough, you look for Royst, and Royst has split, man. Royst is gone. To greener pastures.

DOX
All right, then, damn Royst...

THERESA
(Continuing.)
And he can just dance in and out of the music the way he want to. Anytime he want to.

DOX
We ain't talking about Royst.

THERESA
Then how about the audience? They come in the club, but they don't listen to the music anymore.

DOX
Make them.

THERESA
Used to be you'd get your behind kicked for running your mouth during a set.

SPOON
It's getting to be a drag.

THERESA
See there, Spoon says I'm right.

DOX
(*To* SPOON.)
You amening all this, huh?

SPOON
You think I'd have this f'ing television otherwise?

THERESA
Now they talk through the ballads, man.

DOX
Play so pretty they *got* to listen.

SPOON
Would as soon feed nickels to the juke box.

THERESA
Or look at some silly white man dressed up like a Rooster.

SPOON
Look, you two carry on. I'm going to pretend I'm checking inventory or something.

(*Exits.*)

THERESA
Deserter.

DOX
You were talking about juke boxes.

THERESA
They don't *care* nothing about the music anymore. So why should I kill myself? I'm just one chick. I want to be just like everybody else, that's all. And not give a damn. "Up in the morning, out on the job. . ." And later for the

111

rest of it, man.

DOX
So you gauge yourself by what "they" do? Or what Royst can and we can't?

THERESA
Yeah. And you know why? Because there's more of them than us. And it's easier for everybody than it is for *us*, so why not join them, huh?

DOX
There's no way you could have been around it as long as you have and not know it ain't never been easy. So that ain't good enough. But if it *is* your reason, then maybe you should quit.

THERESA
I told *you* that.

DOX
You're nineteen years old and think you know the world. You can be as irritating as a scratch on a new record. I used to feel sorry for people who didn't have kids. You get your hands from your mother, but your personality— Who do you take after? — Maybe you're really Floyd Tandy's daughter.

All he wanted to be was ordinary. Maybe musicians shouldn't have families—

THERESA
Maybe they shouldn't. And I turned twenty on my last birthday. And who is Floyd Tandy?

DOX
You got my card, didn't you? He was somebody always after your mother.

THERESA
I know Aunt Paulette had to remind you. And if they shouldn't have to have families then why do they?

DOX
What do you *feel* when you play? Don't you feel like the world's not big enough to hold you! Let alone to understand or appreciate or *handle* you. You can't even handle it yourself. Why do you think Bird was so hard on himself? And Billie, and...

THERESA
And on the people that love them?

DOX
Yeah, well, whatever; they knew it was way passed being ordinary. —Maybe it came too easy for you?

THERESA
What came too easy for me?

DOX
There was this kid in the joint. Had to struggle for every inch. I taught him to hear the music, to play it, to feel it, and...

THERESA
And since he had lessons from the Master he's blowing with Duke's orchestra, huh? And that's a lesson for me: if I do the same thing, fame and fortune await me too, huh?

DOX
No. He's dead; an argument with another con about who was the better tenor player, Paul Quinichette or Stan Getz ... Just as he was beginning to learn some rules...

THERESA
So you're saying you don't think I'm ready to go with Ronnie Nichols.

DOX
If I hadn't thought it I wouldn't've talked to him about it in first place.

THERESA
—Oh— I wondered why out of the blue he would send for me—

DOX
(Apologetic.)
Think of it as your twentieth birthday present.

THERESA
You still don't even know when my birthday is.

DOX
I know you come out of my loins, and my woman.

(A confession.)
I don't have a bar, or—*any-thing*— The music's all I've got to give you.

THERESA
What makes you think I want any *thing*?

DOX
You're doing what you're doing for something. I hope it's for more than spite.

THERESA
Spite is for kids, and fools.

DOX
Then which one are you?

THERESA
Why do you think I want to spite you?

DOX
Same reason you married LeRoy. Same reason you didn't write me for the last four years.

THERESA
Why didn't I hear from you?

DOX
　　　(Weak.)
I wrote.

THERESA
"How's school? Hope you're minding Paulette and Spoon. Be good. Your daddy." Talk about sound, they didn't even *sound* like you.

DOX
　　　(At a loss.)
What did you want me to say?

THERESA
>*(Silent.)*

DOX
What?

THERESA
>*(Not a direct answer.)*
Mama was dead. You were in jail.

DOX
>*(Silent.)*

THERESA
Tell me how you were feeling. What I could do for you.

DOX
I had to do it myself— Without putting *more* on you. More than I had—

THERESA
>*(Silent.)*

DOX
Say something.

THERESA
>*(Silent.)*

DOX
So is that it? Because I'm a lousy letter writer?

THERESA
>*(Silent.)*

DOX
You could have written and told me that, you know.

THERESA
            (Reluctant.)
It wasn't just that—

DOX
            (Fearful.)
What?

THERESA
            (Silent.)

DOX
Theresa—

THERESA
            (Blurting. Sharp.)
You let me down, damn it.

DOX
Because of what? I went away? What? Because I what? Tell me.

THERESA
WhenI was little and heard you playing in here and they applauded I clapped too, and thought, That's my daddy. He's the Prince, handsome and charming and sharp. They love the music he makes and they love him. But not as much as me. Mommy doesn't even love him as much as I do.

DOX
            (At a loss.)
Thank you.

THERESA

Think of it as your birthday present. I pretended I was St. Theresa. It was my duty every night to cast my spell so nobody could hurt you...

DOX

The spell wore off. She died.

THERESA

And you just went away. Where I couldn't help you.

DOX

I was holding her hand when she died— And you're mad at me for going off— You lucky I didn't cut your throat and blow my own damn brains out.

THERESA

But all I wanted was for us to be together. With our tears or our grief, our—whatever— Uncle Spoon and Aunt Paul- ette, well I loved them, but they were Ben and Lester's mommy and daddy— My mommy was dead. And my daddy— At first I was really mad at you, man. If I had seen you on the street begging for nickels I wouldn't have given you a penny— Then I was mad at mama for dying and making you think you were all alone. And then one night I heard Aunt Paulette and Uncle Spoon talking. About you. And she said, "Well at least he's got his music—" And I guess I thought you had it, instead of me—

(Long silence.)

DOX

(Moves to bar. Pours himself a drink of liquor.)

THERESA

(She moves to him. Puts her hand on his to stop him from drinking.)

You still didn't tell me what was in the letter I never got.

DOX
I apologized. That was first. For messing up.

THERESA
You didn't...

DOX
(Continuing.)
With your mama, with you— And I said that it's what *you* do that's important. And if you use what I'd done as an excuse to be all full of bitterness, like them cats I was in prison with, then you were learning the wrong message.

THERESA
I wish...

DOX
You've got to keep all that out of yourself, because if you play, and you ain't right, inside, then your sound'll have thorns all over it.— What I always try to do is send them home with pretty on their minds.

THERESA
I wish you'd sent it.

DOX
I didn't have the right.

THERESA
That's all I wanted. To go through it together. And then, at the end *we* would have some—memories—stories.

DOX
Stories?

THERESA
Like you and Uncle Spoon. You and mama. Like Aunt Paulette andMama had. When I was little that was why I wanted to grow up. So I would have stories to tell.

DOX
About what?

THERESA
Sharing. Being happy.

DOX
(Gets horn case & begins to slowly assemble the tenor.)
Yeah— You're a woman now, and...

THERESA
Yeah?

DOX
("OK, I admit it.")
The next generation.

THERESA
(Pleased, but cautious.)
Yeah?

DOX
Maybe even a jazz woman— Like Duke said.

THERESA
He said jazz *is* a woman.

DOX
But not no ordinary one. Me and Spoon was just talking about your mama and Paulette. Neither one of them was even close to being nothing like no ordinary— If you can look me in my face and tell me you've ever done anything where you could feel as good about yourself, and do it with as much style, then I'll get you a husband, a house, a two car garage, and a yard full of petunias and kids, and build a picket fence to go around all of it.

(Music.)
(Presents the assembled horn for her view.)
The horn. Shaped like a snake about to strike. The *tenor*. Seducer. Conqueror. Coleman Hawkins opened it up for all the rest of us. He took it from the um-pah marching band time and made it swing.

Yeah, Bean blew *Body and Soul* so pretty, people still making babies to it. Then tenor number two, Lester Young, leapt in. Yeah, Pres took it next in his gentle hands. And where he skipped along up here, Ben Webster, tenor number three, took it down here, beautifully. Ever beautifully. And that's the whole history of the tenor. Till us. The tenor is the way I tell mine. And that's all it's all about: a man telling his story...

THERESA
Or a woman telling hers—

DOX
("That's right.")
And your mama understood that. And was right there with us. *Ahead* of us sometimes. Telling hers... It was our intention to turn it in-side-out. And we were doing

121

it. And it wasn't no coon show. Wasn't no shuffling, scratching, grinning or shamming. We were a whole new kind of niggers, baby. We walked, dressed, thought, talked, and made music in a way Black men...

THERESA
Black people...

DOX
...hadn't never done before, lady. Not in this country. — And it excited a whole lot of people.

(Music ends.)

THERESA
Excited them, huh?

DOX
That's right.

THERESA
    (Signifying.)
Women especially.

DOX
    (Understanding her tone.)
In their way.

THERESA
All up in your face...

DOX
    (Overlapping.)
You're a musician, you know how it gets... —But I always tried to be careful about giving your mama reason to be suspicious.

THERESA
(Laughs.)
If she'd ever caught you with another woman she'd've killed you, I bet you that.

DOX
(Laughs.)
Don't you think I know it.

THERESA
(Laughs.)
She almost did one time.

DOX
When?

THERESA
(Moods shifts from levity, builds to joy of sharing.)
I heard her and Aunt Paulette laughing about it one time. Said she heard you were fooling around with some waitress or dancer or something.

DOX
Bet she heard it from Floyd—

THERESA
(As the story progresses it is fueled by the laughter and amusement she overheard during its original telling.)
And she decided she was going to catch you in the act.

DOX
That Negro was always telling some lie, trying to turn her against me so he could get next to her.

THERESA
Said she told you she was going home one night, but hid on the floor in the back of the car.

DOX
            (Amused.)
Naw she didn't.

THERESA
After the gig you came out alone.

DOX
I was a married man. Couldn't be seen coming out of a club with a woman.

THERESA
Said you drove to the woman's apartment and went in...

DOX
What woman's apartment?

THERESA
...but by the time she got out you were inside the building, but she didn't know which particular apartment you'd gone into.

DOX
When was this suppose to've been?

THERESA
            ("I don't know.")
So she said she went back and waited in the car.

DOX
Is this for real, or you just making it up?

THERESA
Just like I heard her tell it.

DOX
I can't see Lily hiding in the back seat...

THERESA
That's what she said. Said she waited about an hour for you to come out, fuming all the time.

DOX
Floyd and Paulette, I'll bet you. Paulette figured she couldn't catch Spoon, so...

THERESA
Then she saw you come out and go into a restaurant next door, she said...

DOX
    (Sudden realization.)
To use the phone! A nasty little chop suey joint over on Mack.

THERESA
    ("Right.")
She said a Chinese restaurant!

DOX
I was going to call her! Tell her I was on my way home. I remember that. You may not believe it, but I remember just what you're talking about.

THERESA
Said you were in the phone booth, with your back to the door.

DOX
I was calling home, going to see if she wanted me to bring home some pepper steak. And wasn't getting no answer. And I'm thinking, now where the hell is she? I know she'd told me she was going home—

THERESA
And she...

DOX
No, wait. Let me: dead in the middle of December. Cold! —And you say she was back there for an hour?

THERESA
Plus the time waiting on you to come out of the club.

DOX
No wonder...

THERESA
(*Anxious to continue the story.*)
And she pushed the door in...

DOX
Phone booth with them folding doors— I'm calling home, just like I'm supposed to, and, Blam!

THERESA
Said you looked like...

DOX
Liked to scared me to death! I never did like the east side noway.

THERESA
Said you went to babbling and jabbering...

DOX
I thought one of them crazy east side Negroes... Everybody over there was crazy. And, naw, she didn't push the door, she kicked that sucker in. And all I could see was she was mad, mad as a wet hen. No, ma'am, she-did-not open the door, Richard, she *kicked* it in.

THERESA
She was so mad at you she couldn't talk.

DOX
My right hand to God; *all* I was doing...

THERESA
Mad at herself for sneaking about hiding in the back seat...

DOX
I know it was tight back there...

THERESA
Mad at you for getting inside before she could see where you went.

DOX
...and cold; old Oldsmobile, the heater didn't half work; know my baby was cold. Guess that was the reason she couldn't move fast. I'd just gone by Teddy's...

THERESA
If she'd a gun...

DOX
Who you telling. Boom! "Baby, what you doing here?, I was just calling you. . ." And she's just standing there, jaw tight as Dick's hat band, looking like she was about to explode. I'm totally in the dark, you dig, don't know what she's there for, *where* she's been, *why* she kicked the door in. All I do know is she's got me jammed up in that phone booth; and I better get her out of this Chinaman's joint before she decides to kick something else.

THERESA
I know she was mad enough too.

DOX
Ou bop she bam!

THERESA
A kook a mop!

DOX
And I'm saying, "Baby, don't act up in here." And she's just standing there, her hands on her hips, fuming and shivering. And do you know the only words she spoke?, the only words out her mouth for the next solid week?

THERESA
What did she say?

DOX
Didn't call me baby, nigger, fool, nothing.

THERESA
What?

DOX
Just: "Take me home." And I wanted to say, "That's where you were *supposed* to be."

THERESA
But you thought better of it.

DOX
Yes ma'am. So, we marched on out to the car, just like we were going home from church... And did not speak to me for one week after that. And my right hand to God, that was before you were born—and I swear I didn't know what the hell it was about, till you just told me, right now.

THERESA
I was supposed to be sleep one night when I heard Mama and Aunt Paulette laughing about that. I had to bite the pillow to keep from laughing so they'd know I was eavesdropping.

DOX
Bet you anything it was Floyd— But that time I just went up to have some drinks with Teddy, I don't even remember what we were talking about.

THERESA
And so you were innocent, huh?

DOX
Nobody is innocent, not where I come from.

(Pause. They bask in the moment that has just passed. A more somber mood.)

THERESA
Most fathers would want me to settle down and have grandbabies for them to bounce on their knee. But you, you man, you want me to stay up all night, hang out in funky, smoky bars, where the pay is bad, and cats be hitting on me all the time...

DOX
Builds character.

THERESA
Oh, now I don't have any character either.

DOX
(Serious.)
I want what's best for you.

THERESA
How you get to be an expert on what's best for me?

DOX
(Indicates his heart.)

THERESA
(Serious.)
Do you think my playing's *any* good?

DOX
Yes.

THERESA
But with the pedigree I've got I should be able to make Bud Powell retire, huh?

DOX
   ("Maybe.")
THERESA
In other words, I could be better.

DOX
I think everybody like gets a gift. Everybody don't realize it, or get the chance to develop it. But some—lucky ones do. Now, don't ask me how it's decided, and it's sad when they don't, but it's even sadder when that gift is just pushed aside, out of anger, or ignorance, or fear, or— Anyway, like I was trying to tell you before, for a musician, your sound is the only thing that's *yours*. That very first sound you make is how they know you're alive, and they say, "Yeah, baby, welcome to the world." And when its all over, they bury you, by yourself, no lover, no money truck, no dope man, just you; barefoot, and with a split up the back of your dress.

But what lives is the story you told. And the way you told it. And the sound you told it with. That's it.

And that sound ought to be everything you've seen and felt and learned. All the stories, all the lessons. . . Good and bad. So if it's honest, and its yours, it can't be ordinary, or like nobody elses.

When I listened to your tape you know one of the things I thought: —Lily.

THERESA
You already told me I sound like her.

DOX
It was proof that she was— Like I know the next time I listen to a jam by Bird, or any of the thousand other cats

that he influenced, y' know—

THERESA
You mean it'll be like he's not gone. —And you thought that when you listened to my tape?

DOX
There was her, and there was you. —Ronnie Nichols will be a good teacher for you.

(Music.)

DOX
Don't think I didn't write because I don't love you...

THERESA
(Trying to be light.)
More than your sound?

DOX
(Light.)
No.

THERESA
(Serious.)
Did you love mama more that it?

(Music fades.)

SPOON
(Enters.)

DOX
One fella said the biggest thing wrong with women is that you have to listen to them. The other fella said, Naw, it was that you have to talk to 'em.

DOX & THERESA
(*Move to the bandstand. She begins vamping at the piano as lights go to half on them.*)

SPOON
(*To audience, referring to DOX & THERESA.*)
The Detroit way.

You know where the word jazz comes from, don't you? From a French word—

(*With exaggerated French accent.*)
jazzer. Means to talk, y'know, run it down. Yeah.

And you know why I put music in here in the first place? Because I thought we needed it. I mean I got this joint almost like a gift— Ain't every day one of us gets an opportunity like that. And so, maybe I'll somehow kind of return the favor. Make a club of *our own.* Where we can come and hear our music without a whole lot of bullshit from people running it to make a buck, but not respecting the music, or us.

DOX & THERESA
(*Continue to "blow" throughout.*)
You know I said about Dox cutting Bird: One Friday night it was, and it was a classic.

Bird's blowing over at the Rouge Lounge, and everybody who can't get in there is here, figuring he will fall by after anyway. So, it's tight in here as 13 people under a parasol. And right down front, from the opening set; these two chicks. Two of the finest brown skins I have ever seen in my natural life! Drinking Bloody Marys, and wasn't having to pay for a-one, courtesy of every dude in eye shot of them.

133

And everybody with a horn is in here in the hopes of getting to blow with Bird when, and if, he shows. But Dox is having none of that; is cutting everybody with nerve enough to unpack his axe. Now Lily is on a break, down at the end of the bar, nursing a Coke with just a little ice, and digging Dox teaching school, and these two chicks digging him. I'm behind the bar trying to help Oscar keep up with the orders.

Okay, so we got Dox, eliminating all competition in anticipation of Bird's arrival; we got these two chicks — You know how when a jungle cat stretches, after a nap, and its muscles like be having a rippling tug-of-war with each other, all slow and sleek and powerful; and how, like, silk looks sliding across a nipple; the sound of nylons rubbing together—?—: these chicks, when either one-of-them goes strolling to the Ladies during a break! And we got a primed Friday night full-house— And about 2:30, in flies Bird. Excitement runs through the joint like Castor Oil through a cat. Bird immediately digs what's happening, draws his axe and mounts the stage. The pressure cooker is on. The flame is lit.

House rules have always been, new man calls the tune. Bird calls *Cherokee*, and takes off like Brer Rabbit through the briar patch! And Dox, Brer Fox, is on him! Like a duck on a June Bug, and is not about to be out run or out done. The crowd is shouting, "Blow!"

And that's when these two chicks get to clapping their hands, and one of them starts hollering, "Go, alto, go!" And Bird is digging this chick and is breathing fire and blowing bullets and tearing that little horn up! And when he comes to the end of his solo he quotes, in rapid succession from, *You Came To Me From Out of Nowhere, I'm In The Mood For Love,* and *Now's The Time.* Talking to her.

And right on top of this, almost, Dox comes in with his

solo, which he begins by quoting *All The things You Are,* and *Things To Come,* to this other chick. Then goes into his solo with his ears laid back. Well the other chicks starts hollering, "Go, tenor, go!" And he does! Chorus after chorus after chorus. Then at the end of his solo he rips off quotes from *Embraceable You, You Go to My Head,* and *Lady Be Good,* aimed at this chick, dig it.

Lily was on her second Coke, light ice, and is just digging all this. Everybody else is screaming. It is so hot we've almost got to take turns breathing. The walls were sweating.

After Dox's solo, him and Bird they start trading 16 bars, then 8, then 4, then 16 again, 8, 4, 2. They wore it and everybody in here *out*. Wasn't a dry nothing in the house People were screaming, whistling, stomping their feet. It's New Year's Eve on Benzedrine. And Bird and Dox are standing there like two fighters, Sugar Ray and LaMotta, after a 15-round war, looking down at Misses Fine and Double Fine.

Lily finishes her Coke, winks at me, and moves to the stand to reclaim the piano. Now Lily was known, among other things, for her ability to play long, hard and fast, from her days playing in the churches. She's the new man, right, so she calls the tune. Everybody is expecting another jet, like *Little Willie Leaps,* or one of them other race horses.

But she goes into a ballad. F'ing everybody up! People are thinking, What's happening, man? Even grumbling a little bit. They want blood. They want to see one of these cats hit this wall doing 900. But Lily was cool; like she was sitting in church on Easter Sunday, only thing missing was a little straw hat. Now you know Detroit piano players. They play all of the tune from verse to coda. The Detroit way. And Lily is all over the piano: Art Tatum and

135

Horowitz. But it was an extremely hip crowd and it wasn't but a minute before they recognize what she's playing: *If I Should Lose You.*

Well Bird, leads off, and he's in to it. His little alto kind of resting on his Buddha belly, big sausage fingers — (f'ing drugs had him bloated up) but that don't stop him.

Bird's painting pictures. Watercolors, like down in the art museum: like landscapes. With like a little bird with a piece of pretty bow ribbon in its mouth; the blue bird of happiness, gliding through a fluffy-pink-cloud sky.

Now it's a whole different thing Bird's painting; people grinning like teenagers at the prom. It's orchid corsages on cotton candy dresses. And Bird steps back, as if to say, "Now out-pretty that." And then Dox begins. And it ain't a ballad no more. Lily is comping under him, and it's like she talking, whispering to Dox and there is nobody else in the joint. A woman talking to her man in that Detroit way like they can do. And it ain't a ballad or even a love song, it's grown folks talking. He's standing there with his back to the audience, blowing directly at her and she is playing at looking directly at him! *If I Should Lose You.* And they whispering back and forth.

You might not believe it, but their message was so strong that couples started like easing out two by two, hand in hand. And it wasn't the lateness of the hour that was sending them out of here. I remember it like it was yesterday. Man, I'd give anything to have a tape recording of that night. Make enough off it so my grandkids wouldn't have to work—which would put them in the same category as their daddies.

The two chicks?

(*Laughs.*)

They both left with Bird.

You know— I never heard either Dox or Lily play that tune again. Separately or together. Now they might have, somewhere else, I'm just saying they never played it in here.

> *(Light fades on* SPOON, *up on* DOX & THERESA.
> *they continue their duet as lights fade on them and the end of the play.)*

RIFFS

Riffs

Riffs was first presented by Ron Himes at the St. Louis Black Repertory, St. Louis, Missouri, on March 31, 1995, with the following cast:

T. MIMS .... Allie Woods, Jr.
GROOVE .... William Hall, Jr.
TUPELO .... Erik Kilpatrick
CLAYBORN .... Ron Himes

Director: Ron Himes
Set Design: Felix E. Cochren
Lighting Design: Glenn Dunn
Costume Design: Linda Kennedy
Stage Manager: Tracy Holliway
Technical Director: Steven Stanley

Riffs

CHARACTERS

T. MIMS: retired department-store doorman

GROOVE: retired rhythm & blues & jazz radio disc jockey

TUPELO: retired barber

CLAYBORN: former blues singer

COSTUMES: These are not frumpy old men. Each is concerned with his appearance. Even *if* they are out of style, they do it with style. Each has a hat or series of them.

PLACE: Detroit's North End; metropolitan Detroit suburb

TIME: Whenever

SETS:

ACT ONE: Spoon's Lounge, a bar. Tables or booth with seating for at least four.

ACT TWO: A fast food national franchise type restaurant. Tables or with seating for at least four.

ACT THREE: Thomas Junior's large suburban backyard. Adirondack chairs & tables.

There is no need for the set to be realistic. Evocative & minimal; open space simple; push it on, pull it off.

At all times the dialogue should be presented as musically as possible. A continuous mix of the rhythms of bop, blues and rhythm and blues. It should approximate a jazz fugue, or quartet for four voices doing themes and variations, with rhythmic repeats, i.e., riffs; swinging whenever possible.

Pre-show music should include "Without a Song," by James Cleveland & "Precious Lord," by Hank Crawford, "Straighten Up and Fly Right," Nat Cole; "Caldonia," Louis Jordan.

ACT ONE
SCENE ONE

(SPOON'S LOUNGE. a bar.
T. MIMS, GROOVE & TUPELO
each is dressed in a dark suit, white
shirt & tie.
GROOVE is seated.
TUPELO enters with 3 drinks, as
T. MIMS approaches with newspaper.)

TUPELO

    (Placing drink in front of GROOVE.)

Scotch rocks, for you, Sonny Boy. Vodka-tonic for me.

    (to T. MIMS)

Club Soda for you.

T. MIMS

    (Passing out sections of newspaper.
    To GROOVE.)

Entertainment and features.

    (To TUPELO.)

Front section.

T. MIMS

    (He is left with sports section. Hesitant about
    asking.)

Anybody?

TUPELO

    ("Why you making me say the obvious?")

...Sports was Fleetwood's...

GROOVE

    ("And you know it!")

Yeah—

T. MIMS
> *(Tucking sports section away.)*

Maybe I'll take a look at it later on.

GROOVE
> *(Grateful for this compromise. to T. MIMS, as he cuts out crossword puzzle with pen knife.)*

Crossword for you.

T. MIMS
> *(To audience.)*

We're all retired, in some way or another from one thing or another. Get together every morning. Not here. This is a —special—unusual occasion. Spoon, who owns the bar let us use it this afternoon. We usually meet for breakfast. Read the paper, talk things over, tell a lie or two— That's what we mean about Fleetwood. Telling stories to crack one another up. Fleetwood was the master.

> *(To OTHERS.)*

Being short one member, but having a quorum, I hereby call to order the North End Preservation Association.

GROOVE

Let it be.

T. MIMS

Done

> *(With sports section. To audience.)*

Sports. Belongs to Fleetwood, the absent member. Like Tupelo said. —Guess because Fleet saw everything as a game.

TUPELO
> *(Proposing toast.)*

To Fleetwood...

T. MIMS
Gone...

GROOVE
But won't be forgotten.

(They drink.)

TUPELO
What I hate is there's nothing we can do.

GROOVE
(With reluctant pride.)
We were there.

T. MIMS
And we did what we could.

GROOVE
Fleetwood knew... And he was cool. That was his way.

T. MIMS
Style. Everything he did was trademarked Fleetwood.

GROOVE
His attitude was manicured and creased till he — went out.

T. MIMS
Like a man.

TUPELO
I just hope — when my time...

("...comes I can be his equal.")

T. MIMS & GROOVE
("Me too.")

TUPELO
(Brighter.)

Much brains as Fleetwood had if he'd been white, two weeks he'd've run the world...

T. MIMS
And wouldn't've stood not being black much longer than that anyway.

TUPELO
If that long. The man loved being black. That was all to it.

GROOVE
Broke the mold when they made Fleet.

T. MIMS
Broke the mold, tore down the factory, and busted up the bricks.

GROOVE
Didn't take life serious, that was his secret.

T. MIMS
He had *father*-wit.

TUPELO
Had style and was funny with it.

GROOVE
'Cause he knew everything is funny.

TUPELO
Ain't it.

GROOVE
But when he *told* a story he was serious.

T. MIMS
Serious as when he was working a hustle.

TUPELO
And that just added to how funny it was.

T. MIMS
Never cracked a smile.

GROOVE
But he enjoyed himself.

TUPELO
Always.

T. MIMS
Even when the going was rough.

GROOVE
And saw to you enjoying yours. Remember laughing so hard one time I peed-on-myself.

TUPELO
Remember the story about Blue Benny?

GROOVE
That time, when him and Crackers got into it 'cause Blue Benny got Crackers fired from some job downtown. Crackers was light skinned enough to pass for white was how he got the job in the first place.

T. MIMS
Naw, naw, it started 'cause Crackers owed Blue Benny some money, and wouldn't pay him.

GROOVE
Crackers was the no-paying-est high yellow Negro I ever seen.

T. MIMS
Guess he thought 'cause he looked like a white man he didn't have to pay his debt to Negroes.

TUPELO
That's how Crackers got the job as a bank guard. Passed for white. Was working in the main branch. Downtown. Fooling *all* the white people. Well, Blue Benny heard about it, decided he'd get even for Crackers not paying him his money. Went, stood up in the lobby, and loud talked Crackers.

Say Blue Benny say, "Crackers!? Negro, that you in here with that gun? Better bring your black behind on out of here and quit clowning!" Naturally the manager fired Crackers on the spot!

T. MIMS
You know Benny was Fleet's cousin.

GROOVE
From down there in Mud Flood, Mississippi, where Fleet was from.

TUPELO
Fleet claimed everybody from down there was a relative of his.

GROOVE
He took care of them, whether they was blood or no.

T. MIMS
Fleet had a thing about family.

TUPELO
(Laughing at the memory.)
Blue Benny went through the North End telling everybody about getting Crackers fired, and Crackers jumped Blue Benny that night coming out of the New Villa Bar. Blue Benny took off running.

T. MIMS
Blue Benny was running and hollering, "Let's talk, I don't

feel like fighting you, Crackers."

CLAYBORN
>(Enters during the following. They acknowledge his presence, but continue their involvement with the story. He joins in their laughter.)

TUPELO
But Crackers didn't want to listen; kept on running Blue Benny like Brer Fox in behind Brer Rabbit. Blue Benny still hollering, "Let's talk. I don't feel like fighting."

GROOVE
Benny ran until he was too tired to holler or run anymore.

TUPELO
Say Blue Benny ducked around the corner, picked him up a brick and stuck out his arm out back around the corner. It's so dark Crackers run up on the brick, Bam! Knocked his self out. Say, Blue Benny stood up over him, say, "I told you let's talk. I don't feel like fighting."

CLAYBORN
Have to get some folk's attention before they'll listen.

GROOVE
Hey, Clay.

T. MIMS
Just telling one of Fleetwood's stories.

TUPELO
Clayborn.

GROOVE
Didn't know if you was going to make it by.

CLAYBORN
    (To all, sincere.)
Thanks for inviting me.

TUPELO
And thanks for being a pall bearer...

CLAYBORN
    ("Thanks for asking.")

GROOVE
I'd like to welcome brother Clayborn as an honored guest to the ir-regular meeting of the North End Preservation Association.

TUPELO
Done.

T. MIMS
    (To audience.)
I don't know if he knows or not, but we're kind of auditioning him. For Fleetwood's spot.

TUPELO
Joyce seem to be holding up good.

GROOVE
Joyce is a trooper. She's like Fleet.

T. MIMS
Yeah, Joyce'll be all right. Give her a little time.

TUPELO
And the preacher didn't try to put everybody through the wringer; make you feel like you ought to crawl over in the casket.

T. MIMS
I hate it when they do that. This preacher said what he

had to say and quit.

> **GROOVE**
> *(Laughs.)*

Yeah, and least Fleetwood's funeral wasn't like Clyde Cooper's.

> **TUPELO**

Clyde "Corn Foot" Cooper. Had him some bad feet.

> **GROOVE**

Clyde would cut little razor slits in his shoes to take the pressure off his corns.

> **TUPELO**

Had so many cuts, shoes look like lace slippers.

> **GROOVE**

I remember McSpade Brothers was handling the burial. McSpade Brothers took care of their burial business, in-a-hurry!

> **TUPELO**

That was what Clyde's wife wanted.

> **GROOVE**

Their slogan should've been "We don't fool around, we'll get you in the ground."

> **TUPELO**

You even look sick, McSpade Brothers got a hearse at your door. With the motor running.

> **GROOVE**

Clyde Cooper's funeral was when McSpade got the speeding ticket going to the cemetery. Instead of a funeral procession, looked like the Indianapolis 500 for hearses. Clyde's widow had them hurrying to get Clyde *ditched*, 'cause she was getting *hitched* again that afternoon.

TUPELO
To the insurance agent sold her the double indemnity policy on Clyde.

T. MIMS
(To audience.)
McSpade got 'em there so quick, Clyde was early for his own funeral.

TUPELO
If they *did* kill Clyde, like everybody say, probably what they did was step on one of his feet.

GROOVE
Clyde had some bad feet. He been dead, what we say?, five years?, bet his feet *still* hurting him.

TUPELO
Feet was bad as Bermuda Mohawk was dumb.

GROOVE
That's the truth.

CLAYBORN
Who's Bermuda Mohawk?

TUPELO
Aw, Clay, you was around in them days, I know you remember Bermuda Mohawk.

CLAYBORN
I would remember somebody named Bermuda Mohawk.

GROOVE
He was a menace to his-self and the North End.

TUPELO
Bermuda used to come in the shop get his hair cut.

GROOVE
(Not in response to T. MIMS.)
Fleet was the one convinced me to use *April In Paris* as my theme. Remind me to tell you *that* story sometime.

T. MIMS
(To audience.)
That's pretty much what we do. Lying and signifying. Our way of starting the day. —I'm T. Mims. Was the doorman at Downs & Johnson's Department Store. During its glory days. Before it deserted downtown for the suburbs. —New fella there is Clayborn. Sings the blues. Simple, pat-your-foot-and-nod-your-head-cause-he-telling-the-truth-blues. Over there is Tupelo. Tupelo had a barbershop. Get you a shoeshine, play you a number, find out what was going on. In his day Tupe didn't cut your head and shave you, you didn't consider yourself presentable to be seen in public. Him and Groove go for partners. They think they the funniest thing since white people tried to do the Boogaloo. And Groove. You might remember him from the radio. A rimming and jiving disk jockey. Was rappin' before they called it that. His theme song was *April In Paris*.

T. MIMS & TUPELO
(Begin to hum or harmonize April In Paris *& do raggedly coordinated dance routine behind him.)*

GROOVE
(Into his old radio rap.)
Brace yourselves my kings and queens,
counts and countesses, knights and knaves,
This is your ever-loving Groove on your radio waves.
Playing nothing but bop and blues,
ever-loving good stuff you can use.

So let in the cat and put out Rover
let these grooving good sounds
to help you get over;
help you forget your ever-loving gig
and ever so gently ease your ever-loving wig.

TUPELO & T. MIMS
(Finish theme song with flourish.)

CLAYBORN
That bring back memories.

TUPELO
When we was talking trash...

T. MIMS
And could back it up!

TUPELO
Who say I can't back it up now?

T. MIMS
You say it, if you telling the truth.

TUPELO
So you saying just because you can't "go long" often as you used to, *I* got to speak low?

(During the following, the dialogue can be overlapping, but should always be musical and good naturedly humorous.)

T. MIMS
Negro...

TUPELO
(Continuing.)
You know what that is, don't you? — Trans-ference.

GROOVE
Look out, Tupe*lo*!

CLAYBORN
Tupelo say "trans-ference."

T. MIMS
Transference?

GROOVE
Boy, I remember when you had trouble saying grits, now you talking about some "transference."

TUPELO
That's right. You don't know what it mean, do you?

T. MIMS
Yeah, I know what it mean.

TUPELO
Mean projecting your short comings off onto me.

T. MIMS
You got that off one of them dumb talk shows, didn't you?

TUPELO
Don't worry about where I got it.

T. MIMS
I hate them damn shows.

TUPELO
The truth the truth, where-ever you get it.

GROOVE
And that's the truth.

TUPELO
Just because you can't, don't mean *I* can't— Transference. I'm like Moses coming off the mountain; I bring it to you, you do with it what you will, Sonny Boy.

GROOVE
Hell, couldn't none of us stay twenty-one forever.

CLAYBORN
We all got to admit our best pipe laying days behind us.

TUPELO
You just need some of them pills I used to use.

CLAYBORN
What was them?

GROOVE
Them Red Rooster, power booster ones?

TUPELO
Naw, them Chinese pills.

CLAYBORN
Chinese?

T. MIMS
   (To audience.)
This is one Fleetwood used to tell. Clayborn might not've heard it.

TUPELO
Fleetwood first turned me on to them.

GROOVE
You say they was Chinese pills, Tupelo?

TUPELO
Chinese super-potency pills.

TUPELO
Fleetwood told me to go up there, knock on the door to the tune of *Salt Peanuts,* twice.

GROOVE
(Does the above.)

TUPELO
Say the secret password... "The Shadow knows..."

CLAYBORN
That was the secret password?

TUPELO
(Taps out Salt Peanuts*)*
"The Shadow knows...," and tell the man Fleetwood sent me.

CLAYBORN
Where was the place?

TUPELO
Oakland. Middle of the block between Tennyson and Connecticut.

CLAYBORN
Middle of the block was your shop, the union hall, the five & dime and the watch repair.

TUPELO
I know what was there. Had my shop there, cutting hair damn near forty years...

CLAYBORN
And I played and sang in every joint along there and on the North End almost that long...

TUPELO
I cut every head and know every move you Negroes

made during that time. Coming in my shop is how all of yall met.

CLAYBORN
What I'm saying is I could walk that block in my sleep, and I don't remember no store sold no pills like you talking about.

TUPELO
Up on the third floor.

CLAYBORN
Wasn't none more than two stories.

TUPELO
You had to go in upstairs from the back.

CLAYBORN
 (*Laughing.*)
Yeah, all right, up stairs from the back..."

TUPELO
The guy that run it was —I never could figure out exactly what he was. Mixed.

CLAYBORN
What mixed with what?

TUPELO
Had red hair, like an Irishman, but dark complected — like, you know, like a Mexican or something, one of them. —And he had a glass eye.

CLAYBORN
Aw, hell—

TUPELO
One glass eye.

GROOVE
How you know?

TUPELO
What?

GROOVE
It was a glass eye.

TUPELO
,Cause it was a different color from the other one, and shiny as a marble in a fish bowl. He be looking all around with one eye, but that glass eye was always dead on you! Didn't even blink. Only thing, one time you go in there, it be over here in the right socket, the other eye be the one moving around normal. Next time you go in there they be done switched around!

GROOVE
You would just forget from time to time.

TUPELO
I know what I seen, Sonny Boy.

GROOVE
But still you didn't let that stop you from going in there getting them pills.

TUPELO
Once I knew what they could do?, I wouldn't've have cared if he hadn't had no head, with blue smoke coming out his neck, I'm going up in there!

CLAYBORN
What was they called?

TUPELO
I didn't have to ask for nothing. I'd knock... "The Shadow knows..." Walk in, he'd look up, glass eye

twinkling from one of his sockets, I say "Fleetwood sent me," he'd reach up under the counter and come up with this little box. Chinese writing all over it. Red and black. Gold letters. I pay him and I'm on my way.

("Simple as that, believe it or not.")

CLAYBORN
Okay, now tell me the one about the Easter Bunny.

TUPELO
If you don't believe me, ask Louie.

CLAYBORN
Louie who?

GROOVE
Louie, your dog?

TUPELO
My dog Louie.

CLAYBORN
Ask your dog. Ask your dog what?

TUPELO
About them pills.

CLAYBORN
What your dog got to do with them pills?

TUPELO
I'm about to tell you about the time Louie got a hold of one of them wonder pills.

CLAYBORN
Your lies multiply faster than rabbits.

TUPELO
Louie. I named him after Louie Jordan.

GROOVE
You know Louie Jordan invented rhythm and blues, don't you?

CLAYBORN
(Sarcastic.)
You mean to tell me it wasn't Bill Hailey and the Comets?

GROOVE
(Rapid chatter radio announcing.)
Now, for your ever-loving joy,
here comes Louie Jordan, my boy.
So "Open The Door Richard,"
before he's "Reet, Petite, and Gone;"
we're gonna let him in,
give him a chance to tickle your
ever-loving funny bone.
It's "5 Guys Named Moe,"
and that's no jive,
dig on Louie Jordan and his ever-loving Tympany 5!

T. MIMS
(Singing.)
"Cal-don-ia!, Cal-don-ia!,...

CLAYBORN
"...what make your big head so *hard*!?"

TUPELO
Bam!

T. MIMS
(To GROOVE.)
You programmed some good music, Groove.

GROOVE
Just tried to play the great ones, keep the sounds alive.

CLAYBORN
Even played some of mine. Helped revive my name a little bit.

GROOVE
I program Clayborn, white boys started calling up the station.
      (As WHITE ROCK MUSICIAN.)
"Who was that singing all them blues, *man*?"

CLAYBORN
They covered my stuff, that put my name back before the public. Got more royalties off them than from singing the stuff myself.

GROOVE
You was good.

CLAYBORN
      ("You was saying. . . .")
Louie Jordan, Louie the dog. . .

TUPELO
See, what would happen, it had always been my habit to put Louie out doors them nights when I was planning on wrinkling some sheets —— if you know what I mean.

CLAYBORN
I'm with you.

GROOVE
      (Signifying.)
Once a week every week.

TUPELO
Anyway, so, after I discovered these pills, it got so I was putting Louie out *every-night*.

GROOVE
Was it ever-loving every night, Tupe?

TUPELO
Seven-nights-a-week, Sonny Boy— with Saturday and Sunday matinees.

GROOVE
Them pills must have been kicking!

TUPELO
But what'd been happening *before* them nights when I was putting him out was when he would go visiting the lady dogs in the neighborhood.

T. MIMS
You figured you was getting yours, why not let him get his.

CLAYBORN
    (To T. MIMS*)*
You heard this before?

T. MIMS
I just understand compassion. The reason he put the dog out was *compassion*. Something ain't much of no more.

TUPELO
But it was *so many* lady dogs around there that Louie had been telling them he was sorry, but he couldn't take care of all of them. But he was claiming it was my fault 'cause I wasn't letting him out often enough.

CLAYBORN
Louie was woofin'.

GROOVE
Dig it, which took the pressure off him, you see.

CLAYBORN
Yeah, I see what you saying, Louie the dog was talking trash when he knew he wouldn't have to prove himself, because you wasn't giving him the opportunity.

TUPELO
But when I started taking them pills, and was putting him out *every* night...

GROOVE
He found out his eyes was bigger than his appetite.

TUPELO
("That's right.")
So, Louie took to watching me. See if he could figure out how, just how the hell I'm handling the strain of this new seven-day-a-week schedule. I be reading the paper like I wasn't paying him no mind, and look at him all of a sudden; catch old Louie eye-balling me every time!— So, one evening — see, I'd take one of my pills just before dinner, so that way just about the time Roberta finishing up the dishes — one of them little boys would kick in, Bong!, and start to do its stuff.
As if to wife, with sexual connotation.)
"Oh, Roberta dear, are you about through in the kitchen?"

GROOVE
And would she lay that dishrag down, Tupe?

TUPELO
Every evening, Sonny Boy! —But this one time I made a mistake and dropped one of 'em on the floor.

T. MIMS
Nervous.

TUPELO
Louie was on it like Satan on sin!

163

(*Threatening* LOUIE.)
"You swallow that pill and it's to the dog pound you go!"
—He looked at me as if to say, "I just *got* to know if these bad boys'll work for me too. Putting *me* out every night. . .

T. MIMS
Couldn't blame him. Lot of pressure on him.

TUPELO
That's what kept me from killing him about my pill.

T. MIMS
Compassion, you see.

TUPELO
Well, he got a drink of water to wash it down. And I let him. Son of a gun shot out of there with his tail straight out!

GROOVE
How long was he gone?

TUPELO
Two weeks. Come back, was scraggly, scrawny, and walking lap legged. His ears was drooping and his tail was dragging. Dragging, but wagging!

T. MIMS
Know he was a happy dog.

TUPELO
Looked happy as a Harlem hooker during a Shriner's convention. Tail wagged in his sleep. —So, Clay, you stop on by there and ask Louie if I ain't telling the truth about them pills.

CLAYBORN
Like he wouldn't lie to back you up.

(THEY *laugh*.)

GROOVE
Well, when I go I want yall to promise have me cremated, like Moms Mabley say, make sure I get hot one more time, anyway.

CLAYBORN
(*To* T. MIMS)
You know what you remind me of?, sitting there doing that crossword puzzle. My grandfather.

GROOVE
Clay sound like he getting ready to play the dozens on his-self.

CLAYBORN
Naw, I'm talking about back home when I was a kid. When my grandma was quilting. Sewing together pieces of scraps of stuff we had worn out and couldn't afford to throw away. Quilting relaxed her. I knew that even though I was just a little knee-high.

TUPELO
My mama made piece quilts, too.

CLAYBORN
Man, she put them colors all together, that cloth be jumping like good Saturday night jazz! Run all that Jim Crow-take-low craziness clean off for awhile.

GROOVE
Called them crazy quilts.

TUPELO
White folks ones called 'em crazy. Made plenty sense to us.

GROOVE
Help you make it through the night.

> (*THEY* laugh.)

TUPELO
> (*To T. MIMS*)

You been working them puzzles since you first started coming in the shop.

T. MIMS
> (*With edge.*)

Because they're the way life should be; a challenge, but fair, an answer to every question. You get one answer, even a simple one, that helps you to get another one.

TUPELO
> (*Picking up on T. MIMS tone.*)

Like you say, like life ought to be.

GROOVE
Way life ought to be. You know what little Langston said to me the other day?

T. MIMS
> (*To audience.*)

Little Langston is Groove's grandson. Eight going on fifty-four.

GROOVE
Me and him was rassling with his math homework...

T. MIMS
> (*To audience.*)

Little Langston went through some tough times with his daddy, Groove's son, before Groove took the little fella in. Groove raising him by himself.

GROOVE
He say, "Groove..."

T. MIMS
(*To* CLAYBORN.)
Groove don't let little Langston call him grandpa, do you Groove?

GROOVE
Makes me sound too much like some old man. So we working on his math. That's his toughest subject. Mine too. Anyway, "Groove," he say, "I'm just a little boy." I say yeah. He say, "It was real tough when I was living with my daddy." I say yeah. He say, "How come I had to go through all *that,* and have to worry about this math too? This how life going to always be?" And he was serious. I wanted to laugh and cry at the same time.

CLAYBORN
Tough telling a kid life ain't fair.

TUPELO
But he's come a long way the two years he been with you.

GROOVE
When I took him, little cat was mad at the world, and had every reason to be.

TUPELO
When Groove first took him the little cat fought in school every-day.

GROOVE
I was in the principal's office so regular had my own desk. "This how life going to always be?" I didn't know what to answer him.

T. MIMS
Like I got a question I don't have an answer to.

CLAYBORN
What?

T. MIMS
About Tom Tom.

CLAYBORN
Your son. Thomas Junior.

T. MIMS
I call him Tom Tom. His mother always hated that. Insisted on calling him Thomas. Like somehow that made him less black.

TUPELO
   (To CLAYBORN.*)*
Boy stepping in tall cotton. *Good* j-o-b with Down's & Johnson. Same place T. Mims worked. —Like father, like son. . .

T. MIMS
Doorman a little different than executive.

CLAYBORN
Fleet said you and Thomas Junior just getting back together.

T. MIMS
Mostly since his mother died.

TUPELO
About a year ago.

T. MIMS
He grew up with her.

TUPELO
Got a nice house out there on Grande Maison Lake.

T. MIMS
Was a time we couldn't move out there.

GROOVE
Couldn't sell, rent or lease to Negroes.

T. MIMS
It was in the ordinances.

TUPELO
Ain't in 'em now.

T. MIMS
 (*Continuing, see in the irony.*)
And Downs & Johnson's led the way out there...

TUPELO
 (*Continuing, seeing the other side of the irony.*)
And now Thomas living out there, and working high up in the company developed the sub-division and built the mall; led the way out there.

T. MIMS
And killed downtown in the process.

TUPELO
He's a grown man, making more money than all of us together in our best days.

T. MIMS
Making money ain't got nothing to do with being a man.

TUPELO
I'm just saying...

T. MIMS
"Just saying" nothing.

TUPELO
You know what I'm saying...

T. MIMS
How much money we made was the standard, wouldn't none of us be men.

GROOVE
   (To T. MIMS, the peace maker.)
What Tupe meant...

T. MIMS
I know what he meant. And I know what is. We all provided...

TUPELO
That's right.

T. MIMS
... in-spite-of. In spite of them same type of white men we worked for, and Thomas working out there at Down's & Johnson *with*.

TUPELO
Well ain't that progress?

GROOVE
That's all Tupe's saying...

T. MIMS
You saying he grown...

TUPELO
Yeah. And I *meant* you can't raise him again. He who he is.

GROOVE
        (Peace maker. to TUPELO.*)*
You don't get but one chance to raise 'em. My roguish son taught me that. T knows that...

T. MIMS
I don't care how old he is, or how much "take home" he take home, or where home is. I'm talking about *who* he is.

TUPELO
He's who you made the way for him to be. For 30 years you opened doors for the mamas and daddies of the ones he working with...

GROOVE
So Tupe saying you ought to be proud.

T. MIMS
I'm so proud I keep popping the buttons off my shirt. But proud don't have nothing to with it.

GROOVE
        (Peace maker.)
T, what Tupe is saying is, you don't get them middle-of-night, desperation, phone calls from Thomas...

TUPELO
From or about him...

GROOVE
...like I do from little Langston's daddy.

T. MIMS
        (To GROOVE*)*
I didn't mean...

GROOVE
Desperate to borrow some money... desperate for bail

money...

T. MIMS
You keep talking about money...

GROOVE
          (*Continuing.*)
You get sick...

T. MIMS
Un huh?

GROOVE
I ain't wishing it on you.

T. MIMS
I hear you.

GROOVE
Thomas Junior is going to look after you.

T. MIMS
I believe it.

GROOVE
I can't say it about my own son, is what I'm saying.

TUPELO
That's what I'm saying. Thomas Junior ain't no trouble.

T. MIMS
          (*To* GROOVE.)
But you got your second chance with little Langston.

TUPELO
          (*Continuing.*)
Your Thomas Junior ain't no trouble.

T. MIMS
Not *that kind* of trouble...

TUPELO
So you ought to be proud.

T. MIMS
You talking about pride in what he's done.

TUPELO
You saying you *ain't* proud?

GROOVE
He ain't saying that.

T. MIMS
I already said I'm proud. I'm saying I didn't do it for the money he could make. And, naw, he ain't never been the kind of trouble you talking about. And I'm thankful for that. What I did I did so he could be a man.

TUPELO
He three times seven, and then some.

T. MIMS
   (With edge.)
I don't measure no man by his age, or what he *got*. — I'm talking about what he *is*. We ain't here because what Fleetwood *had*. But-who-he-was. You see what I'm saying?

GROOVE
I see what you saying.

T. MIMS
We, what —? — *Loved* Fleet...

GROOVE
Yeah—

TUPELO
Okay—

T. MIMS
Because he found a way to be black, *and* be a man —

GROOVE
I hear you.

(To TUPELO.*)*
You hear what he saying.

T. MIMS
...without being an imitation white man... A black mole playing a role in a white hole.

GROOVE
And letting them forget what they put you — us through.

CLAYBORN
And more than that, forgetting they can do the same thing to him at the drop of a hat!

T. MIMS
("I glad you finally see it.")
Thank you!

TUPELO
And you worried Thomas...?

T. MIMS
Might be flying so high he can't see the ground.

CLAYBORN
You don't know if he slicking them, you saying...?

T. MIMS
Or him-self?

CLAYBORN
He playing the game, or the game playing him?

GROOVE
Is he the trickster?, or the tricked?

CLAYBORN
The duper, or the duped? The player?, or the patsy?

T. MIMS
That I don't know. . . I can't *read* him. We talk, he don't even know when I'm being sarcastic or ironic. — And then there's his wife. I don't know what to do, but I know I've got to do something.

GROOVE
 (*To* CLAYBORN.)
Thomas' wife says she's a descendent of Jefferson David's wife's family.

CLAYBORN
That Civil War Jeff Davis?

GROOVE
The head confederate. *President* of the South.

CLAYBORN
And she's descendent from him.

GROOVE
Claims to be.

T. MIMS
His third cousin or something, and one of his slaves.

CLAYBORN
Don't know if I'd brag about that or not.

GROOVE
But what's her point?

T. MIMS
Can't talk to her five minutes she don't work it in the conversation.

CLAYBORN
Jeff Davis, huh? Wonder what Fleetwood'd have to say about that?

(*THEY* laugh.)

TUPELO
I'm going to miss him.

GROOVE
"*We're*" going to miss him. — Gentlemen, it's time for me to sign off. Got to do my math homework. Then pick up little Langston from school.

(*To* CLAYBORN.)
Thanks again, Clay.

T. MIMS
Brother Groove, do you have closing remarks for us?

GROOVE
(*Composing as he goes.*)
Today we buried our friend, the good Fleetwood,
we knew he was — leaving,
we did all what we could.
We'll remember his spirit through all our grieving,
and Hell yeah, we'll miss his style and his jive,
but the North End Preservation Association,
will keep his memory alive.
T. Mims got a problem concerning his ever-loving son,
when we meet tomorrow we'll figure out
what should ever-loving be done.

T. MIMS
Thank you Brother Groove.

CLAYBORN
Let me get that sports section nobody don't want it. Like to stay up on the baseball standings.

T. MIMS
It's all yours.

OTHERS
>*(Pleased.)*

TUPELO
>*(Raises his glass, proposing a toast.)*

To Fleetwood, one more time.

>*(Pause. They drink.)*

T. MIMS
I hereby suggest the adjournment of the North End Preservation Association.

TUPELO
Let it be.

GROOVE
Done. — Gentlemen, see you in the morning.

TUPELO
Guaranteed.

GROOVE
Guaranteed.

>*(CLAYBORN, TUPELO & GROOVE exit.)*

T. MIMS
>*(To audience.)*

That's what we do.

(We hear April In Paris.)
**END OF ACT ONE,
SCENE ONE**

ACT TWO

(Next morning.
Restaurant.
Each more casually dressed than previously.)

GROOVE
  (To TUPELO.*)*
Coffee, black.

TUPELO
Thank you, Sonny Boy.

GROOVE
  (To CLAYBORN.*)*
Coffee black.

CLAYBORN
Right the first time.

GROOVE
  (To T. MIMS.*)*
Tea, no sugar.

T. MIMS
  (Passing out newspaper. To GROOVE.*)*
Entertainment and features.
  (To TUPELO.*)*
Front section.

CLAYBORN
  (To TUPELO.*)*
I can tell you what the news is: somebody killed somebody, politicians arguing about my money, and the white folks still ahead.

T. MIMS
  (To CLAYBORN.*)*

179

Sports.
I hereby call to order the North End Preservation
Association...

TUPELO
With special guest.

>   *(Nod towards* CLAYBORN.*)*

OTHERS
Here, here.

T. MIMS
Having a quorum, we will proceed.

GROOVE
Let it be.

T. MIMS
Done.

T. MIMS
>   *(To* GROOVE.*)*
Any opening remarks?

GROOVE
>   *(Reciting.)*
Yesterday we buried our main man,
today, his spirit with us,
we meet again.
Our order of business is to
help T. Mims figure what to do now
about his son, living high on the sow,
makes *big* money, and he ain't dumb,
just seems to've forgot where he come from.

T. MIMS
Thank you brother Groove.

GROOVE
Talked to Joyce last night.

CLAYBORN
Me too.

T. MIMS
Yeah, she sounded okay. — You know, I could hear *April In Paris* playing in the background while we were talking.

GROOVE
Yeah — maybe that was what put it on my mind — Fleet, when he was telling a story, was like a jazz musician.

TUPELO
How you mean?

GROOVE
Listening to him was like digging a Lester Young solo.

T. MIMS
Pres with Basie.

TUPELO
Dig it.

GROOVE
Soft. Easy. But swinging.

T. MIMS
Swinging!

TUPELO
Fleet was something, man.

GROOVE
Best I ever heard. He'd get in the middle of a story and you could swear you could hear like the whole Basie band riffing up under him.

T. MIMS
Amen.

TUPELO
Was like that when Martin Luther King was speaking.

T. MIMS
Don't forget Malcolm.

CLAYBORN
Both them boys could stir up a meeting.

GROOVE
You know how come Malcolm wasn't big as King when they was alive? Malcolm started off asking colored people to give up that pig.

CLAYBORN
Big mistake!

T. MIMS
Malcolm was talking about discipline.

CLAYBORN
Average Negro figured, he didn't have much of nothing in the first place...

GROOVE
They was both after the same thing, just was going about it in different ways.

TUPELO
Apples and oranges.

GROOVE
Dogs and cats.

CLAYBORN
Never cared much for cats. Dogs. Dogs know what's

happening; how to act, how to show appreciation. But cats?, naw.

TUPELO
Never know where you stand with a cat. But with a dog...

CLAYBORN
Except for a Chihuahua I knew one time. Name of Pep. Woman owned him dressed him in a little cashmere coat, and a baret cocked down over one eye. He was mean.

TUPELO
You want to talk about mean, mention a Doberman pincher.

GROOVE
   (Laughing.)
Ask Bermuda Mohawk about them Dobermans.

CLAYBORN
I *still* don't remember Bermuda Mohawk.

GROOVE
Cats ain't affectionate enough for me. Step on Fido while you stumbling in four in the morning; *still* glad to see you.

TUPELO
But cats?, naw. I'm feeding you, you got to show me more signs of affection than going to the bathroom in a box.

GROOVE
   (At window.)
Look a-there.

TUPELO
What?

T. MIMS
Where?

TUPELO
That boy out there, going through the garbage.

GROOVE
Look at that.

TUPELO
Tough as times was when I was a kid I never dug through no-body's garbage; and Sonny Boy, if I hadn't been cute as I was, I believe they'd've let me starve. *Still...*

GROOVE
Ought to just go 'head get them a regular job...

CLAYBORN
You got a job to give him?

TUPELO
Going through other folks garbage ain't nothing for no man to do.

T. MIMS
Maybe it's so they can be free and independent.

CLAYBORN
It's tougher now than when you was young.

TUPELO
That's a lie.

CLAYBORN
What's sad is how young they are.

GROOVE
What they looking for anyway?

CLAYBORN
In their twenties some of them. How somebody that young fall that low that fast?

GROOVE
In our day you had to be our age before you got to bum status.

T. MIMS
It's the pressure on them. America don't need them like it used to. No foundations to lay, no crops to harvest, no war to fight.

GROOVE
But if they ain't' begging, going through the garbage they robbing and stealing.

T. MIMS
I never thought I'd say this, but we might've had it easier.

TUPELO
Can they collect enough to buy that crack?

GROOVE
The trash disturbers are winos. The ones doing all that breaking and entering and mugging, them're your crack-heads.

CLAYBORN
You know why, don't you? Where all this 20th century wild west comes from— Cow's milk.

T. MIMS
What?

TUPELO
He say cow's milk.

CLAYBORN
Cow's - milk.

T. MIMS
That's what I thought he said.

CLAYBORN
Cow's milk. Soon as mothers quit nursing 'em on breast milk, and went to exclusively feeding all this animal milk?, they went to acting like animals. All these poor women got to give to their babies in the first place is themselves. Some human contact.

TUPELO
They call it bonding.

T. MIMS
There you go with that talk show babble again.

CLAYBORN
But these young mamas don't even give that. Baby come in a brand new world, don't even get to suck a tit. Mama too worried about getting somebody to love them. Baby just something to turn into a toy, and parade around in a stroller. Till the novelty wear off. Then sit it in front of a TV, stick a bottle full of animal milk in its mouth and go on about her business. Baby sit his little ass there sopping up all the television foolishness, and sucking in that hyped up animal mess. . . No wonder they don't care about nothing. You got to treat a human baby like a human baby.

T. MIMS
Otherwise won't have no compassion.

TUPELO
That's right.

GROOVE
These young boys so disconnected they'd kill God for sneezing.

CLAYBORN
No mother's milk; that's what's wrong. Young girls just do what convenient for them, don't think what's best for that baby. Now tell me I'm lying.

TUPELO
Can't.

GROOVE
You right.

CLAYBORN
Mother's milk...

T. MIMS
All these kids need a dose of discipline. That was my point about Malcolm!

CLAYBORN
Bet them boys going through that garbage don't even know who Malcolm X was.

TUPELO
Would know he hadn't ask 'em to give up that pig! And talking about pig put me in the mind of China Red.

GROOVE
Sure do. China Red could ever-loving bar-b-que him some pig. China Red. Negro looked like a Black Chinaman dipped in lye.

TUPELO
But he could smoke him some ribs, Sonny Boy.

GROOVE
He would just set up on the corner there where Reverend Sweet had his church.

TUPELO
Reverend Sweet, the Sweet Reverend. What was the name of that low-down Negro's church?

GROOVE
Don't remember. Remember it was the corner down from Shorty O's. Name'll come to me.

CLAYBORN
Reverend Sweet. I remember that name. What ever happen to him?

GROOVE
Bermuda Mohawk is what happened to him. He was a menace to his-self and the North End.

TUPELO
China Red had him a barrel drum cut in half, and some baby buggy wheels on it and some screen wire, you know. That was his pit.

GROOVE
And a beat up old lawn chair...

TUPELO
Would set up there in front of that church...

GROOVE
He never did work.

TUPELO
Didn't believe in it. But he would scuffle around till he had enough to buy the meat and charcoal, then Red would get busy.

GROOVE
Once that smoke got to drifting around that was his advertising. He didn't have to do nothing else! Couldn't cook them ribs fast enough.

TUPELO
First sell he made he send get him a bottle of Comet's Tail muscatel. His first one of the day.

CLAYBORN
That Comet's Tail was some nasty stuff!

GROOVE
Man, hush!

TUPELO
It was sweeter than Mogan David, thicker than homemade molasses...

GROOVE
And would go though you like greased Castor Oil.

CLAYBORN
Professional drinkers couldn't handle that Comet Tail hotch.

GROOVE
Had a reputation worse than Jim Crow.

TUPELO
They say it was so bad, if it didn't blind you, would make you shoot yourself.

CLAYBORN
That Comet's Tail almost made me give up drinking. Negro slipped and give me some of that Comet's Tail wine one time, big old jelly-jar glass full. Was in a after hours joint over there on the east side, I was playing and singing the blues; this gal was in there to see me. I'd met

her on the Clairmount bus going over to see about some Stacy Adams shoes a boy was selling at wholesale. I got to talking to her on the bus there. We hit it off pretty good, and I told her where I would be at, so naturally she come by one night to see me, you see. I'm on break and the bartender set a glass in front of me. I ain't paying no attention. My mind is on this girl, and I drank it, bottoms up!, before I knew what I was doing. It went down smooth enough, but before it got where it was going felt like somebody had grabbed me by the throat, cold-cocked me with a crow bar, and kicked me in the ass all at the same time. My eyes wouldn't focus, I couldn't get my breath, and I had a twitch in my left foot. I went to sweating like I working the afternoon shift in August at Henry Ford's foundry.

TUPELO
Them foundry boys worked!

T. MIMS
Yes, sir, they earned their money.

CLAYBORN
Last thing I remember, Nat King Cole was singing "Straighten Up and Fly Right," on the juke box. When I woke up I was sitting propped up against the fence at Elmwood Cemetery. In my underwear and socks. Everything else, including the girl and my guitar, was gone!

TUPELO
Everything?

CLAYBORN
What did I say?

GROOVE
What did you do?

CLAYBORN
Walked home.

TUPELO
Walked home?

CLAYBORN
Now I *might* could've flagged a cab and talked him into carrying me home, but I didn't even try. I was so disgusted with me I wanted to teach my damn fool self a lesson. So, like I say, that Comet's Tail wine almost ruined me for drinking, or chasing after strange women.

TUPELO
Almost.

CLAYBORN
  ("Almost.")
That's why I don't see how nobody could drink that mess on a regular basis.

TUPELO
China Red thrived on it.

GROOVE
First sale, he got him a bottle; and he was a happy, nappy head red Negro then.

TUPELO
  (To GROOVE.)
You know who else drank that mess, don't you?

GROOVE
Who?

TUPELO
Bermuda.

GROOVE
Bermuda Mohawk.

TUPELO
Bermuda Mohawk. He sure did.

GROOVE
I know it.

CLAYBORN
(Pause.)
I *still* don't remember Bermuda Mohawk.

GROOVE
He was the hard-luck-est, low down-est son of a gun ever breathed air in the city of Detroit.

TUPELO
If luck was sugar, Bermuda couldn't've sweetened a spoonful of tea.

GROOVE
If common sense was soapy water, Bermuda couldn't've bathed a flea. And drank that Comet's Tail long as he could get it.

TUPELO
He was a menace to his-self and the North End.

GROOVE
Except for that one time.

TUPELO
That's right. Bermuda went for Indian.

CLAYBORN
Blackfoot?

GROOVE
Foot, face and ass.

TUPELO
Claimed on his granddaddy's side he was a West Indian Indian. Say that's where the name Bermuda come from. Claimed his grandmama was full blooded Mohawk.

GROOVE
Tried every way he could think of to keep from being a plain old Negro.

TUPELO
One while Bermuda had me shaving his head with just a patch down the middle. Mohawk style.

T. MIMS
That's what kept him from having good sense, spent so much time trying to keep from being an ordinary Negro till it ruined his judgement. — Like Tom Tom's wife.

GROOVE
You remember his biggest mistake of all?

TUPELO
His biggest mistake, and the first positive thing he ever did.

TUPELO
Cameron Street. Christmas Eve.

CLAYBORN
What yall talking about?

GROOVE
("Yes.")
But there was another time too. The time with the monkey.

T. MIMS
>*(To audience.)*

You see what's happening, don't you? You know what they getting ready to do.

TUPELO

When was that?

T. MIMS
>*(To audience.)*

Lie.

GROOVE

You remember about the dancing monkey.

TUPELO

I don't remember that.

GROOVE

You didn't hear about that?

TUPELO

Don't remember.

GROOVE

You'd remember if you had. Panhandler's monkey.

T. MIMS
>*(To audience.)*

They getting ready to tell lies on innocent animals now.

TUPELO

Naw—

GROOVE

Panhandler named Six-Mile Willie. Had a parrot, Pinochle Polly, and a monkey that danced.

T. MIMS
You lying.

GROOVE
If I'm lying, I'm flying.

T. MIMS
Ladies and gentlemen, fasten your seat belts. We are in for a rocky ride.

GROOVE
And wore a top hat all the time.

CLAYBORN
Who?

GROOVE
Huh?

CLAYBORN
The top hat.

GROOVE
Six-Mile wore the hat...

CLAYBORN
Six-Mile was the panhandler?

GROOVE
Six-Mile Willie.

CLAYBORN
And the monkey danced.

GROOVE
While the parrot whistled.

TUPELO
I don't remember nothing about this.

GROOVE
Monkey's name was *Master* Mumbo Jumbo.

CLAYBORN
Master Mumbo Jumbo.

GROOVE
They panhandled mostly around Eastern Market.

TUPELO
Did?

T. MIMS
> *(To audience.)*
He say "Did?" like they didn't work this out before hand.

GROOVE
Six-Mile Willie, Pinochle Polly, the whistling parrot, and Master Mumbo Jumbo, the dancing monkey. And they made pretty good money.

TUPELO
Did?

T. MIMS
> *(To audience, mimicking.)*
"Did?"

GROOVE
Especially on Saturdays; day folks go down to get fresh vegetables and meat. That monkey could dance.

T. MIMS
> *(To GROOVE.)*
I suppose "Master Mumbo Jumbo" did a tap dance?

GROOVE
Did a dance to whatever kind of music Pinochle Polly the

parrot would whistle. And she could scat-whistle just like Ella Fitzgerald doing *How High the Moon.*

(Demonstrates.)

TUPELO
Could he Charleston?

GROOVE
Could Mohammed Ali run his mouth?

TUPELO
I'd like to see a monkey do the Charleston one time before I die.

T. MIMS
(To audience.)
Isn't that everybody's dream?

GROOVE
Master Mumbo Jumbo done it. You missed it.

TUPELO
Damn! I missed Tiny Tim's wedding too.

GROOVE
Six-Mile Willie wore that top hat all the time, summer and winter. It was his trademark.

CLAYBORN
The monkey and the parrot should've been trademark enough.

GROOVE
Kept the parrot up under the top hat when they wasn't working, collected handouts in it when they were. Anyway, Bermuda was down there one time, picking up some peaches for Shorty O.

TUPELO
That's right, 'cause he worked for Shorty O.

GROOVE
Drove a truck, picking up fruit for Shorty O to make that moonshine.

TUPELO
Sure did.

GROOVE
That's when Bermuda saw Six-Mile Willie and his dancing monkey.

TUPELO
That make sense.

T. MIMS
(To audience.)
Yeah, right.

GROOVE
End of the day Six-Mile Willie, Pinochle Polly1 and Master Mumbo Jumbo, the monkey, go down the alley at Orleans to the bank there on Gratiot.

T. MIMS
Before they put the expressway through so the white people could get out of town quick.

GROOVE
Six-Mile was saving up for another monkey. Had to save; couldn't get a loan.

TUPELO
Couldn't he get a co-signer?

GROOVE
Master Mumbo Jumbo was the only somebody Six-Mile

Willie knew with any money. But the fact the monkey was making more money than most Negroes during that time, didn't hold no sway with the loan officer.

TUPELO
Saving to get another monkey, huh?

GROOVE
Yeah, a girlfriend and dancing partner for Master Mumbo Jumbo. The little hairy son of a bitch stayed horny, and was getting hard to live with. Got so Six-Mile was scared to leave Master Mumbo Jumbo alone with Polly.

T. MIMS
(To audience.)
Imagine the off-spring from that union! Get something can hang by its tail, eat bananas, talk about your mama, and then fly its signifying behind on off?

GROOVE
This one time Bermuda delivered the peaches to Shorty O. Then he got him a jug of that Comet's Tail Wine. Went back down to the market. Sipped away the rest of the day, watching Six-Mile, and them do their show and collect money. Night fall. Market closes. Six-Mile and Master Mumbo Jumbo heading for the bank. Polly up under the top hat. It's dark, right. Bermuda run up behind them in the alley there, grabbed Master Mumbo Jumbo, threatened to blow its monkey brains out Six-Mile don't hand over the money.

CLAYBORN
That's low down, mug a man's monkey.

T. MIMS
(To audience.)
The lie these two Negroes telling; *that's* what's low down.

GROOVE
Bermuda played like he had a pistol, all it was was his hand in his pocket. But Six-Mile didn't know that. He handed over the day's receipts, and Bermuda run off down the alley.

TUPELO
That was cold.

GROOVE
Naw, that was when Bermuda's trouble started.

TUPELO
Cops caught him, huh?

GROOVE
Worse than that. But he did end up empty handed and in jail.

TUPELO
Like always. That Negro was a menace to his-self and the North End.

GROOVE
Except for that one time.

But this time, before he could get to the other end of the alley, Crackers, with shoe polish on his face as a disguise, jumped out from behind a trash can and told Bermuda to stick 'em up.

Bermuda jumped bad. Showed his hand-in-his-coat-pretend-like-he-had-a-pistol-pistol. Crackers showed Bermuda his real-pistol-in-his-hand-pistol, then run off with *Six-Mile's* money *and* Bermuda's wallet and clothes, except for them six buckle goulashes he wore all the time.

CLAYBORN
You didn't say nothing about Bermuda wearing

goulashes before.

TUPELO
They was kind of his trademark.

GROOVE
Anyway, Bermuda, naked as a jaybird, went straight to the Police station, to file a complaint on the Negro mugged him. By that time Six-Mile and his menagerie showed up to file their complaint about being mugged. Bermuda couldn't identify *his* mugger, except that he was dark skinned, and smelled like Kiwi...

TUPELO
That shoe polish...

GROOVE
...but *Master Mumbo Jumbo*...

TUPELO
...The monkey...

GROOVE
...give the police a positive i.d. on *Ber-muda!* They loaned him some prison over-alls and locked his butt up.

TUPELO
Sound like what they call a precedent setting case.

GROOVE
Bermuda fought it up to the Supreme Court.

TUPELO
Master Mumbo Jumbo hired an NAACP lawyer and won the case.

GROOVE
It was in JET.

TUPELO
Yeah, Bermuda was a menace to his-self and the North End, whether he was drinking that Comet's Tail Wine or not.

GROOVE
But China Red was the one, drinking that Comet's Tail and cooking his bar-b-que.

T. MIMS
Bar-b-que... Some things come and go... Y'know, like fads, like hula hoops, pet rocks...

CLAYBORN
Disco, bell bottoms...

T. MIMS
But some things hang tough. Like bar-b-que. Always been. The pig sustained us till we could do better.

CLAYBORN
Amen.

T. MIMS
Between snouts, chops and trotters, bacon, ribs, ears and tails, — not to mention chit-ter-lings and maws, well, gentlemen, the pig brought us a long way. We can-not forget the pig.

GROOVE
>(Raises glass, proposing a toast. Begins slowly, composing as he goes.)

After our doctor's latest diagnosis,
of everything from trichinosis
to cirrhosis
we can fuss,
'cause nothing we liked was good for us,
whether a swig, a cig, being a nig

or a meal of Mr. Pig.
M.Ds say it clogs the passages to our heart,
and we mustn't eat if we're smart.
We say, doctor, doctor, all that may be true
but when we started eating it
it was all that we could do.
Necessity was the mother,
choices?, we had no other, we was bereft
so however bad it was for our hearts
we ate it cause that was all left
after the white folks eat all the good parts!

    TUPELO
Right on! for Mister Pig.

    CLAYBORN
Prince Porker.

    GROOVE
Herr Ham...

    TUPELO
Señor Sow...

    CLAYBORN
Summed it all up in-a-nutshell. Hadn't been for us using every last bit of pig- parts to survive, America wouldn't be what it is today. Pig was the fuel that gassed our tank...

    GROOVE
Preach!

    CLAYBORN
...and our energy is what fueled America; allowing it to *prosper.*

    GROOVE
Teach!

CLAYBORN
That's how white folks got so far ahead.

GROOVE
Help him, tell the story, Lord!

CLAYBORN
So the pig is part of our heritage from our parents, who had nothing but gumption and grit. But between them and pig parts, they brought us a long, long way.

GROOVE
(Amening.)
A long way.

T. MIMS
That's my point! That-is-precisely-my-point. We can't forget them. Some of our daddies might've left when the pain and strain got too much...

CLAYBORN
Some of our mamas protected us too hard...

TUPELO
God bless 'em.

CLAYBORN
But we can't forget 'em.

GROOVE
Like we can't forget our kids.

T. MIMS
And we can't let them forget us, and what it cost us to be us.

GROOVE
And the lessons we learned getting to be us.

TUPELO
Think all separates them from being white is skin color.

GROOVE
How they get so dis-connected so quick?

CLAYBORN
White folk's education for one thing.

T. MIMS
And ZAP!

CLAYBORN
They get amnesia of the soul.

GROOVE
Bet it took longer to turn an African into a slave.

CLAYBORN
One semester in a college more effective than four or five generations of branding, starving, chains, and hard labor. Brains be washed, fluff dried and starched lily white.

T. MIMS
Think 'cause they got an automobile cost more than the block of houses where I was raised, history don't apply to them.

GROOVE
Think they're immune from the madness of racism.

CLAYBORN
Got boys think they playing music, don't know nothing about the blues.

T. MIMS
They have forgotten the pig.

CLAYBORN
And cow's milk.
Went through all the doors we opened...

T. MIMS
Then closed 'em behind them!

CLAYBORN
What if he needs to come back through?

TUPELO
He need something to remind him.

T. MIMS
Hot damn! Out of the mouths of babes.

TUPELO
Who you calling babe?

T. MIMS
I'm getting a brain storm. Need a little time to set it up. First thing Monday morning I'm picking you up in the truck.

GROOVE
What truck?

T. MIMS
Truck full of bricks.

TUPELO
Bricks?

T. MIMS
You deaf too? Bricks. And wear your work clothes.

TUPELO
How come every time somebody else get an idea, *I* got to put on *my* work clothes?

T. MIMS
I hereby suggest the adjournment of the North End Preservation Association.

TUPELO
Let it be.

GROOVE
Done.

END OF ACT TWO

ACT THREE

*(Following Monday morning.
THOMAS' backyard.
There is a stack of bricks or cinder blocks on a flatbed hand truck. We get the sense of a patio & a spacious yard. There are sturdy Adirondack-like lawn chairs & tables.)*

T. MIMS

(During the following he begins, through trial & error, to lay bricks in what will serve as the foundation of the bar-b-que pit.)

T. MIMS
I opened doors winter, summer, spring and fall. For thirty years. When I started at Down's and Johnson the few blacks that worked inside had to be off the floor and stay out of sight during business hours, except elevator operators. That's what Tom Tom's mama was doing when I met her.

CLAYBORN
Thirty years.

T. MIMS
"Yes ma'am, Mrs Hoity Toity. Welcome to Down's & Johnson, Mr. Muckety Muck."

CLAYBORN
I remember you; green cap, long coat. You was sharp.

T. MIMS
"Good day now, and thank you for shopping at Down's & Johnson." Shopping at Down's & Johnson meant something.

CLAYBORN
It was something. — Before they moved out of the city.

T. MIMS
Didn't just move out; *abandoned*.

CLAYBORN
Took the money and run. The American way. Wasn't the same for blues joints to sing in after that.

T. MIMS
Final coffin-nail in down town. And malls don't need doormen. I was still drinking then.

CLAYBORN
Hell, everybody was.

T. MIMS
Try to wash the taste of all those "Yes ma'ams" out my mouth.

CLAYBORN
Singing the blues and drinking turned into drinking and *having* the blues.

T. MIMS
Got pretty heavy when she left and took Tom Tom.

CLAYBORN
Just left.

T. MIMS
Left nothing but bills and dust balls.

CLAYBORN
Daddy don't count in court.

T. MIMS
So she could spend full time turning my son into Clarence Thomas or Dan Quayle... I tried to stay in touch, use to send him books and records. I wanted to school him as much about Baldwin and Malcolm and

Monk as she was filling him up with Mozart, Nixon and Hemingway, or whoever.

CLAYBORN
Naw she didn't...

T. MIMS
She had me fooled from the gitty-up. Played it like she was the princess of Conant Gardens. Called things "quaint." Talked "proper", vase was "vahz," tomatoes was to-mah-tos.

CLAYBORN
High class...

T. MIMS
Thought she was... Thought her daddy must be a doctor or something, turned out the Negro shoveled coal for Mistile Brothers Coal Company.

CLAYBORN
(Singing.)
"Thought she was high class, but that was just a lie... I'

T. MIMS
(Laughs.)

CLAYBORN
Big Mama Thornton! "You ain't *nothing* but a hound-dog..."

T. MIMS
"'Ain't never chased a rabbit..."

CLAYBORN
"...and you ain't no friend of mine." Elvis Presley took it, didn't he?

T. MIMS
Black face in white face.

CLAYBORN
Then forget where he got it.

T. MIMS
Believed he was the King, forgot he was just a Mississippi redneck...

CLAYBORN
You forget, you get lost.

T. MIMS
Cut off.

CLAYBORN
You get lost, *that's* it...! Elvis sing any of your songs?

CLAYBORN
Had 'nough white boys singing my tunes make up a new Tabernacle Choir. But naw, not Elvis.

T. MIMS
Too bad, or you could've profited something back, off *him*, he had.

CLAYBORN
Maybe that's what Thomas doing. Being a white minstrel in black face?, maybe.

T. MIMS
—May-be—

CLAYBORN
Like Elvis stole our stuff by 'being' us, maybe Thomas' doing it back to them.

T. MIMS

Is, I hope he fooling them as well as he fooling me. when you watch him walk, from the back you can't tell if he white

(Demonstrates.)

or black.

(Demonstrates.)

And he knows more about the PGA than the N.B.A.

CLAYBORN

But you and him get along okay?, you know, better than Groove and little Langston's daddy.

T. MIMS

There's some — feelings. Not a lot of understanding yet. I'm letting him come at his own speed. . .

CLAYBORN

You're being cool.

T. MIMS

Trying to.

CLAYBORN

Like fishing. . . You can battle a fish into the boat, or you can finesse him. . .

T. MIMS

You fish?

CLAYBORN

Cools me out. Fleetwood went with me a couple times.

T. MIMS

I don't have the patience.

(By this time T. MIMS is satisfied with the dimensions of the foundation he has laid. He

locks to CLAYBORN *who gives his nodded approval.)*

CLAYBORN
But you're being cool, with Thomas.

T. MIMS
I *think* I'm doing okay.

CLAYBORN
And it's been like that since she died, Fleetwood say.

T. MIMS
Yeah. He made the effort.

CLAYBORN
That's a good sign. Had to come from him.

T. MIMS
'Cause I couldn't force it, y'know. Couldn't let him know how glad I was.

CLAYBORN
When *he* wanted it; you had to be cool.

T. MIMS
He'd got all the stuff I sent. The books, records, all that.

CLAYBORN
Kept it all too, I bet.

T. MIMS
All I want's for him is to keep his guard up; not believe his strength's in his zip code, or the title on his door.

GROOVE
(WHITE MAN.)
What you Negroes doing anyway?

T. MIMS & CLAYBORN
(Startled.)

TUPELO & GROOVE
(Enter with fast-food carry out bags.)

TUPELO
Look to me like you tearing something down and getting ready to steal the bricks.

CLAYBORN
We been building a bar-b-quo pit, by-our-selves.

GROOVE
And look to be doing a hell of a job, don't let us stop you.

TUPELO
Where you get the bricks, this quick?

T. MIMS
I didn't know Fleet forty years and not learn something.

TUPELO
They ain't hot are they? I don't do my best work handling hot merchandise.

T. MIMS
You do your best work getting out of work.

GROOVE
We'll follow your lead. You the boss, Boss.

(Pulling items from bags. To CLAYBORN.)
Coffee, black.

CLAYBORN
Thank you.

GROOVE
(To T. MIMS.)

Tea, no sugar.

T. MIMS
I hereby call to order the North End Preservation Association. Special suburban session.

GROOVE
Let it be.

TUPELO
Done.

GROOVE
This way out here, ain't it?

TUPELO
Bet ain't nobody going through the garbage out here.

GROOVE
Bet they don't even *allow* garbage out here.

TUPELO
There was any trouble out here it'd be a week before the news got back to "the ghetto."

GROOVE
It's so far out here we lost reception of my old station on the radio. Couldn't get nothing but classical music and stock market up-dates.

T. MIMS
    (Signifying.)
That why yall late?

TUPELO
We late 'cause I been chauffeuring school-boy here.

GROOVE
Had to go to a parent teacher breakfast.

TUPELO
Tell 'em, Sunny Boy.

GROOVE
(With pride.)
Little Langston got a "satisfactory" on his deportment report; first time. And, 3 A's, and 2 B's in his scholastic stuff. Including a B in Math.

T. MIMS
(Requesting "five.")
My man...!

GROOVE
(Giving "five" all around.)
Acorn don't fall far from the mighty oak.
And you know what my theory is on stupid is, don't you? Follow some ignorant kid home, somebody ignorant will answer the door.

TUPELO
Same go for ugly.

(They have begun work again Mostly T. MIMS & CLAYBORN, they work well together, anticipating each other's moves and needs. They take occasional breaks, separately & together. GROOVE joins in, but primarily as an assistant to T. MIMS & CLAYBORN. TUPELOL'S greatest contribution is staying out of the way, which he does as obtrusively as possible.)

TUPELO
All right then, what you building?

T. MIMS
This a bar-b-que pit.

TUPELO
Thomas Junior want a bar-b-que pit, couldn't you've just bought him one of the Weber portables?

T. MIMS
I don't know that he even *wants* one.

TUPELO
Then why go to. . .?

T. MIMS
Explaining something to you's like trying to sweep marbles up a wall. The point ain't the *thing*. — It's the message behind it.

TUPELO
You want to send him a message, what about a telegram?

CLAYBORN
Ain't what you do, it's the way you do it.

TUPELO
Want to explain that?

CLAYBORN
It's a lesson for Thomas Junior, but it ain't like T's sitting him down telling him lynch stories like we got told. It's like T's giving him a quilt, like my grandmama give me. Wouldn't take nothing for that old quilt.

T. MIMS
Now if you ain't going to contribute nothing, get out the way so men can work.

TUPELO
I ain't working on nothing I ain't seen the plan for.

T. MIMS
We don't need a plan, we going to improvise, Sonny Boy.

TUPELO
Plan, "Sonny Boy," is for somebody want to start out building a bar-b-que pit, and don't end up with the Leaning Tower of Pizza.

T. MIMS
Them I-talians had a plan for the Leaning Tower of Pisa, for all the good it did them. They'd contracted the job out to brothers the thing would be standing up straight. The proof is in the pit, my friend. It ain't the plan, it's the man, and I am the man.
(Indicating his head & heart.)
And up here and in here where my plan.

GROOVE
Sounded like me, didn't he.

TUPELO
Every pit I ever built had a plan. And just 'cause your head hard as a brick don't mean you can model a bar-b-que pit on it, Sonny Boy.

T. MIMS
T. Mims begin making a bar-b-que pit, T. Mims end up with a bar-b-que pit! And you ain't told me how many pits you built.

TUPELO
How many?

T. MIMS
How many?

TUPELO
How many bar-b-que pits have I built?

T. MIMS
Tell me.

TUPELO
This week?, or in my life time?

T. MIMS
A figure.

TUPELO
What's your point?

T. MIMS
I mean it must be in double figures. The way you talk, they must call you Johnny Bar-B-Que Pits. You must got bar-b-que pits in back yards from Mississippi to Massachusetts. From Maine to Montana.

TUPELO
I built a few.

T. MIMS
That ain't no number.

TUPELO
How many women you had?

T. MIMS
I *know* you ain't saying you built many pits as I had women.

TUPELO
   (Over end of above.)
I'm saying you can't remember the exact number...

T. MIMS
   (Over end of above.)
You saying you built many bar-b-que pits as I had women?!, then you a brick-laying-mortar-forming-son-of-a-brick-layer!

   (They both laugh.)

TUPELO
I still say it'll be a miracle you get this baby built with-out a plan.

GROOVE
(*Laughs.*)
Speaking of miracles...

TUPELO
I know what you going to say.

GROOVE
What?

TUPELO
Bermuda

GROOVE
... that time with Bermuda and the Cameron Street Christmas Eve Story.

T. MIMS
(*To audience.*)
They must phone each other up at night get their routine together for the next day.

CLAYBORN
The Cameron Street Christmas Eve Story?

TUPELO
The *one time* he ended up doing something positive for his-self and the North End.

GROOVE
The Cameron Street Christmas Eve Story.

TUPELO
You have to tell 'em about Shorty O first.

T. MIMS
(Taking a break. To audience.)
Here they go again.

GROOVE
You remember what year it was?

TUPELO
I remember times was real tough.

CLAYBORN
(Taking up T. MIMS' work slack.)
That could be any time.

TUPELO
Particularly tough.

T. MIMS
During the Depression?

GROOVE
I don't go back that far. This was later than that, but times was still tough.

CLAYBORN
On what they called Black Monday, the start of the Depression... the day the stock market crashed?, my daddy's business was wiped out, and he almost got killed.

GROOVE
How?

CLAYBORN
He was working on Wall Street...

T. MIMS
(To audience.)

They got Clayborn lying too.

TUPELO
The closest your daddy got to Wall Street was a railroad depot in Mississippi.

GROOVE
What was he?, a stock clerk?

CLAYBORN
Naw, he was working *on* the street— shining shoes.

GROOVE
And what happened?

CLAYBORN
A stockbroker that had lost all his money, jumped out the window.

TUPELO & GROOVE
(Together.)
Landed on your daddy's shoe box. . .

CLAYBORN
Just missed killing him, otherwise I wouldn't be here today.

GROOVE
Man jumped must've been white, black folks don't kill themselves about money.

TUPELO
Might kill somebody else about it, but not themselves.

GROOVE
The time of the Cameron Street Christmas Eve Story was one of those times when everybody was broke. Wasn't nobody in that whole neighborhood working!

TUPELO
Except Shorty O, and his people worked for him. Rumor was Fleetwood banked Shorty O.

CLAYBORN
Where else was Shorty going to go for a business loan, First National?

T. MIMS
White folks wasn't giving loans to legitimate black businesses, know they wasn't going finance a combination gin mill after hours joint.

GROOVE
Anyway, Shorty O had a whiskey still in that middle house there.

TUPELO
1100 block of Cameron.

GROOVE
A two family flat.

TUPELO
The still, where he made that bad liquor, was up in the attic.

GROOVE
Only house in that block didn't never have no snow on the roof in the winter time.

TUPELO
And the only house where the electricity was on.

GROOVE
Shorty O the only one could afford to pay the bill.

TUPELO
Except for the church.

GROOVE
Reverend Sweet's church. Down at the other end of the block.

TUPELO
On the corner.

GROOVE
Outside where China Red cooked his bar-b-que.

TUPELO
Except for the church everybody who had electricity was renting it from Shorty O.

CLAYBORN
Doing what?

GROOVE
Shorty O had the monopoly on the electricity renting business.

TUPELO
He was renting electricity to everybody else in the block.

T. MIMS
Wait.

TUPELO
Renting electricity.

GROOVE
Had extension cords strung up and down the block.

T. MIMS
You lying.
(To audience.)
You know better than this.

GROOVE
Naw he ain't, neither. Had extension cords running out his windows on both sides.

TUPELO
And out the back, through back yards, over fences, down the alley...

CLAYBORN
I believe it.

T. MIMS
I don't. Now what about the Cameron Street Christmas Eve Story?

TUPELO
What about it?

T. MIMS
That's my question to you, what about it?

TUPELO
We coming to it.

GROOVE
So I was saying, Shorty O's house had so many wires coming out of it till it look like a bad-hair process taking a recess.

TUPELO
Was the sole source of electricity in that block.

GROOVE
Except for the church down at the other end of the block, across the street.

CLAYBORN
Reverend Sweet's church, outside where China Red did his bar-b-queuing.

T. MIMS
Go 'head on.

GROOVE
Now Shorty O wasn't just making money off that moonshine and electricity.

TUPELO
Had damn near many hustles as extension cords.

GROOVE
Was open for business *twenty-four* hours.

TUPELO
'Round the clock.

GROOVE
Year 'round.

TUPELO
Wasn't closed but two days a year.

GROOVE
Christmas Eve and Christmas day.

TUPELO
Had his whiskey still up in the attic.

GROOVE
You could get you a woman on the second floor.

TUPELO
But you couldn't go down in the basement.

GROOVE
Worth your life to try to.

TUPELO
That was common knowledge.

T. MIMS
>*(To audience.)*

There's going to be a lie about that basement too. You watch.

GROOVE
First floor was for gambling. Poker in the parlor, craps in the dining room.

TUPELO
Bar was in the kitchen. That's where the basement door was. Shorty O had a sign on it say:

>OFF LIMITS!
>TO *EVERY* DAMN BODY.
>THIS MEANS YOU!!!!!
>MANAGEMENT NOT RESPONSIBLE
>YOU TAMPER WITH THIS DOOR

Same sign was posted on the back door leading to the basement from the back yard.

T. MIMS
>*(To audience.)*

See. Just wait.

GROOVE
Wasn't nobody fool enough to try and go down there, neither.

TUPELO
With one exception.

CLAYBORN
Bermuda Mohawk.

GROOVE
Negro was a menace to his-self and the North End.

TUPELO
Except this one time.

GROOVE
Tell 'em about the water taps in the kitchen.

TUPELO
Shorty O had the still in the attic hooked up to the kitchen plumbing.

GROOVE
How it would work, you bring a glass in there, and hand it to that gal standing there by the sink.

TUPELO
Along with the money. She hold it up under the faucet run you off a drink.

GROOVE
The "hot" tap was the stuff directly out the still.

TUPELO
The "cold" tap was whiskey he'd made two or three days before.

GROOVE
"Aged."

TUPELO
Pay the girl, tell her what you want, she draw it from the proper tap. You go on 'bout your business.

GROOVE
The girl would put the money in a dumb waiter. It would go on down to the basement.

TUPELO
Same in every room. The dealers on the first floor and the girls on the second floor would accumulate so much

money, drop it in a slot in the floor by the wall, it would drop down to the basement.

GROOVE
So as far as everybody knew the basement was loaded.

T. MIMS
(To audience.)
Didn't I tell you? They're building up to it.

TUPELO
Say Shorty O had a vault down there bigger than the one at the First National Bank.

GROOVE
Say he couldn't hardly close the door so much money in there.

T. MIMS
(To audience.)
They can't even tell a lie without it being a super lie.

TUPELO
Kept two dogs. Two Doberman pincers.

CLAYBORN
I wouldn't have a Doberman. Too inbred. Like rich white people, ready to snap any second.

GROOVE
A male and a female. Named David and Bathsheba.

TUPELO
They patrolled the backyard 24-hours a day.

T. MIMS
Excuse me. Is this *still* the Cameron Street Christmas Eve Story story?

GROOVE
Cameron Street Christmas Eve Story story.

T. MIMS
You think It'll be next Christmas Eve before you tell it?

TUPELO
You want to hear it or not, Sonny Boy?

CLAYBORN
Tell it.

GROOVE
So, *in-spite* of all that, Bermuda come up with his crazy idea of breaking into Shorty O's basement and robbing that vault.

T. MIMS
    (To audience
    "See, what did I tell you.")
I've been knowing them too long...

TUPELO
So Bermuda Mohawk he'd get the truck, go down to the Eastern Market, get a load of fruit, deliver it to the back gate. Then some of Shorty O's inside people would haul the fruit in the house to make that moonshine. Bermuda would stay in the alley.

GROOVE
Bermuda wasn't never allowed into the back yard. He stayed with the truck the whole time. While the dogs stood guard. But somehow he decided his best shot at that money was through the back door.

CLAYBORN
Where the two Doberman pincers...

TUPELO
David and Bathsheba was. While the others was taking the bushels of fruit into the house Bermuda would slip them dogs a piece of meat.

GROOVE
That he had got from one of the packing houses while he was down to Eastern Market.

TUPELO
Throw the meat over in the yard, and say, "Nice doggies."

CLAYBORN
Getting on their good side.

GROOVE
They'd take it, snap it up and not say a word, not *wag* their tails, nothing. But they didn't bark.

TUPELO
Bermuda did this 'bout a month, never had a woof out of 'em.

GROOVE
Started right before Thanksgiving.

TUPELO
Two pieces of meat over the fence, "Nice doggies."

GROOVE
Started at Thanksgiving, figuring a month was plenty time to get friendly with David and Bathsheba before Christmas Eve.

CLAYBORN
Which was when Shorty O was closed you say.

TUPELO
Christmas Eve and Christmas Day.

GROOVE
The one time of the year Shorty O wasn't open.

TUPELO
Christmas Eve and Christmas day. All other times you could go in there, get what you wanted.

GROOVE
Bermuda knew this.

TUPELO
Everybody knew it.

GROOVE
But everybody else had better sense than to take advantage of it though.

TUPELO
Nobody *ever* accused Bermuda of being smart.

GROOVE
Whether he was drinking that Comet's Tail wine or not.

CLAYBORN
You say he was a menace to his-self and the North End.

TUPELO
Except this one time.
And yes, he was dumb, but determined.

GROOVE
Where he had short comings in one area...

TUPELO
He'd make it up with deficiencies in another.

GROOVE
That night, Christmas Eve, Bermuda went into action.

TUPELO
Little light snow *was* falling.

GROOVE
It was the picture-perfect Christmas Eve. Bermuda throwed them dogs some meat over the fence. They took it. Same as always. Never made a sound.

TUPELO
Watched, kind of nonchalant, while Bermuda climbed over the fence.

GROOVE
He *"Nice* doggied" himself right over into the back yard.

TUPELO
David and Bathsheba sat right there, and didn't say a word.

CLAYBORN
That's how them Doberman pincers do. Any other dog would've kept up so much racket Bermuda wouldn't've dared even try to get in. But them Doberman's got their own style.

T. MINS
    (To audience.)
They like a woman about to dog her man for something she's decided he did wrong.

TUPELO
They just sat there and watched him till Bermuda dropped down over in the yard with them.

GROOVE
Then he threw them another piece of meat. "Nice doggies."

TUPELO
Everything was fine.

GROOVE
So he thought.

TUPELO
Right.

GROOVE
The minute he made a step toward that house David and Bathsheba went to work.

TUPELO
On him like a school of piranha's on a hippo steak.

GROOVE
Got between him and way he got in, and *undressed* him! Got him out his clothes quicker than a $400 French whore. Cut *every* stitch off him. Didn't bark, didn't growl, didn't make a sound.

TUPELO
All that Negro had on when he got *back* over the fence was his hat and them six buckle galoshes he wore.

CLAYBORN
Say they was his trademark.

GROOVE
Dog had even cut them and his socks, down to level with that bottom buckle! And then sat there and laughed at his bare ass.

TUPELO
Bermuda hit that alley moving.

GROOVE
That's when his trouble started.

TUPELO
He got tangled up in them extension cords coming from Shorty O's.

GROOVE
Bermuda is a bare-assed centipede caught up in a web of electric wires.

TUPELO
The boy *was* snatching and rassling and pulling; busy as a bucket of gophers on speed.

GROOVE
Going at it like Joe Louis after Max Schmelling in their second fight.

TUPELO
That was a fight!

>   (*During the following, under, as raspy voiced RING ANNOUNCER.*)

"...and a left to the head by Louis, and a right to the jaw, another left to the head and a right and a left, by Louis who is raining blows!..."

GROOVE
Joe hit that Nazi so quick, hard and frequent they had to look at it in *slow motion* to count the blows.

CLAYBORN
Joe whupped that white man like he had stepped on his mama's bad toe and hadn't said "'Scuse me, Mrs. Louis, ma'am."

T. MIMS
Joe's strength was coming from all of us. Every colored man, woman and child in the U.S., *and* Ethiopia.

TUPELO
That's how Bermuda was mixing it up with them wires. But the more he struggle the worse it get.

GROOVE
In his desperation to get loose he goes to snatching plugs from sockets. Lights start to go out.

TUPELO
Christmas tree lights, lamp lights.

GROOVE
Every light in the neighborhood that was hooked up to Shorty O's.

TUPELO
Which was all of them.

GROOVE
—went out. It's a dark and silent night all up and down the 1100 block of Cameron.

T. MIMS
(To audience.)
They forgot about the church down the street.

GROOVE
It was so dark snowflakes couldn't see how to hit the ground.

TUPELO
Folks looking out to see what the Hell's happened to the lights.

GROOVE
But can't see nothing, because it dark as Baptist preacher's funeral suit.

TUPELO
Bermuda's trying to lay low; deciding whether he wants to suffer frost bite, or be caught by what was rapidly growing into an angry mob.

GROOVE
Then, like the star in the heavens... Bermuda spots the *only* light in the night. The lights from the church on the corner.

TUPELO
Reverend Sweet's church.

GROOVE
Outside, where China Red bar-b-qued his ribs.

TUPELO
Twinkling like the star of Bethlehem. 'Cept Bermuda wasn't no wise man from the East.

GROOVE
Bermuda heads for it, tiptoeing in a low crouch, and hugging himself like a python around Tarzan.

TUPELO
Meanwhile, in the church, Reverend Sweet's running his all night Christmas Eve service. And it's guaranteed he's going to keep 'em in there till he's got enough money for his Christmas bonus.

GROOVE
Reverend Sweet was his name. "Reverend Sweet the sweet reverend," was his claim to fame.

TUPELO
"The Holy, Healing, Hands-On Evangelist."

GROOVE
He was Sweet Chocolate before he first come to the North

End. Was a big time pimp down in Ohio. Was so good at it, he'd pulled all the other pimps' women into his stable. They formed a pimp posse. Run Chocolate out of Cincinnati. Middle of the night; nothing but the clothes he had on, and a copper back pocket watch with a silver dollar dial. The watch always run about 15 minutes slow, but Sweet had a sentimental attachment to it. because his father had sold it to him on his death bed.

TUPELO
Sweet took the pimp's revenge as a sign. Retired from the pimping business. Come up here and went to work on the line at Ford's. Midnight shift. Claimed it was at lunch that first night he got the call to preach.

GROOVE
Them stamping machines made many Negroes call on God.

TUPELO
Sweet started in a little store-front on Oakland off Harmon.

GROOVE
Within six months couldn't get in there on Sunday for the women! Lined up. Good looking women, too. Within a year they had got him a program on the radio, a house on Boston Boulevard had five bathrooms, a four-car garage, Cadillac, and that church there on the corner down the street from Shorty O's joint.

TUPELO
"The Good Time All Denominational House of Salvation, Deliverance and Love Temple, Reverend N. T. Sweet, the Holy, Healing, Hands-On-Evangelist, Presiding." That was the name of it.

GROOVE
Reverend Sweet was set on giving Prophet Jones and Daddy Grace a run for their money.

TUPELO
Was well on his *way*.

GROOVE
Anyway, Sweet was preaching his Christmas sermon. Had taken his text from *Romans*. Chapter 13. Verses 6 and 7.

TUPELO
"...pay ye tribute also; for they are God's ministers... Render therefore... tribute to whom tribute *is due*..."

GROOVE
Meanwhile, outside, the night air was full of buckshot and bullets being squeezed off in the general direction of whoever it was had put folks in the neighborhood in the dark.

TUPELO
Bermuda, cold, confused and confounded, headed for the light; see if there was any room in the inn, so to speak.

GROOVE
So, just as Reverend Sweet's whipping his congregation into that final offertory spirit, before he took the exit offering and unlock the doors to let them out the church —that's when Bermuda invented streaking. He hit the front door of that church hard as a flying box of concrete. It was man versus door. Something had to give. It was the door. Bermuda busted it loose from the hinges and is barreling down that center aisle, naked, with so many splinters and ice sickles on him look like a porcupine. And he's hollering "Save me, save me!"
Sister Sarah, the head of the usher board, and stationed at the foot of the pulpit facing the congregation, saw

Bermuda first. Giving no consideration to her personal safety, but concerned only with protecting her beloved Reverend Sweet, Sister Sarah leapt into action.

TUPELO
Sarah wasn't no more than five-one, ninety something pounds. But wiry, with plenty heart. Before she got religion Saran caught her husband, Tap City Teddy in bed with big Mattie Fairbanks. Little Sarah'd made Tap City jump out a second story window and had big Mattie wedged up in the broom closet, and was assaulting her with a whistling tea pot. Till the police kicked in the door. It took the four of them, and a back-up unit to get the cuffs on Sarah and rescue Mattie.

GROOVE
Took the Fire Department twice that to get big Mattie unwedged from that broom closet.

TUPELO
Finally greased her hips down with a can of Crisco. Pried her loose with the Jaws of Life.

GROOVE
Anyway, Sister Sarah hit Bermuda with cross-body block, and was sitting a-straddle him, giving him a lecture on the dress code of the Good Time All Denominational House Of Salvation, Deliverance
And Love Temple.

TUPELO
And Reverend N. T. Sweet, the Holy, Healing, Hands-On-Evangelist? Now I don't know if he thought it was them Cincinnati pimps finally catching up to him, or what, but Sonny Boy, before anybody knew it Sweet was not there. Sweet was gone!

GROOVE
In the wind, with the wind. That was when the neighborhood stampeded through the front door, in hot pursuit. It was dark, like we say, so nobody hadn't actually *seen* Bermuda to know it was him they'd been chasing. First thing they see as they rumble in is little Sarah sitting on buck naked Bermuda and wagging her finger in his face.

TUPELO
That just confirmed the weird goings-on some of them had suspected all along.

GROOVE
Next thing they noticed the rear door of the church flapping back and forth like the wings of a albatross trying to get airborne in a wind storm.

TUPELO
Reverend Sweet had hit that back door going out doubling how Bermuda had hit it coming in! The neighborhood vigilantes run on through the church. After who they *thought* had put them in the dark.

GROOVE
They must've picked up Sweet's footprints just outside the back door. Fresh snow and all. But, to this day, nobody will say for sure what happened to Sweets. Don't know if the mob caught up with him?; if he took off flying?; if God pulled him up?; Satan pulled his sinning soul down, or *what!* Nobody won't say.

TUPELO
A conspiracy of silence. But it was the last anybody on North End heard of Reverend Sweet, the sweet reverend.

GROOVE
Only trace left was his robe, with the copper back watch

in the pocket.

TUPELO
All because of Bermuda Mohawk.

GROOVE
So his part in helping get rid of that jackleg Sweet was the *one* favor he did for the North End.

CLAYBORN
What happened to Bermuda?

GROOVE
Him and Sister Sarah got married. Sarah showed him the joys of being a black man. Last I heard he was a deacon.

TUPELO
Sweet's congregation got another preacher. Changed the name of the church. Even converted China Red.

GROOVE
Call it the North End House of Holy Smoke & Bar B Q.

CLAYBORN
All that ruckus, wonder everybody didn't go to jail. Charge 'em with being lewd and nude, disturbing the peace, inciting to riot, breaking and entering, public nuisance, drunk and disorderly...

TUPELO
All the stuff they'd charge a brother with when they couldn't think of nothing else.

CLAYBORN
Yeah, it used to be open season on you colored boys.

T. MIMS
Thomas don't know nothing about that.

GROOVE
Kids now-a-days; it ain't in a video or on a computer they don't know it.

T. MIMS
They don't know they faced with the same thing we were. Just more subtle. The same old soup, but served in China bowls.

CLAYBORN
Open season every season. They limit us to a pair of six-league boots to walk in, then give us egg shells to walk on.

T. MIMS
But we done it.

TUPELO
Didn't we.

CLAYBORN
Yeah we did...

T. MIMS
(Presenting the completed bar-b-que pit.)
Gentlemen.

OTHERS
(Inspect it thoroughly.)

TUPELO
(Huffs & puffs on it like the Big Bad Wolf.)
It's a bar-b-que pit, all right.

T. MIMS
(To others, signifying, as he loads leftover materials on flatbed.)
Did we need a plan?

TUPELO
You got lucky.

T. MIMS
"Lucky" for folks don't know what they doing.

CLAYBORN
Yes, sir, gentlemen, we built us a bar-b-que pit in these suburbs I

TUPELO
Didn't we!

T. MIMS
  (*To* CLAYBORN.)
And you, my brother, are a brick laying —

CLAYBORN
Careful—

T. MIMS
Brother!

CLAYBORN
I accept your well deserved praise.

T. MIMS
  (*To* TUPELO.)
And you...

CLAYBORN
What you lay Tupe?, two bricks?

TUPELO
Management don't actually do what you call hands-on labor.

GROOVE
Ain't your fault if Thomas don't understand what the pit is about. You certainly put it there for him.

CLAYBORN
Like with Crackers that time, and Blue Benny, making him run into that brick; have to get some folks' attention before you can talk to 'em.

T. MIMS
What we have built here today may be little noted, and may not be long remembered, but it ain't just a bar-b-que-que pit, it's a letter from home.
  (Holding up cup.)
I christen it the Fleetwood Memorial Bar-B-Que Pit.

OTHERS
Right on!
  (They pour libation on it. They drink. pause.
  They begin to gather things, preparing to exit.)

T. MIMS
  (Passing out newspaper. To GROOVE.)
Entertainment and features.
  (To TUPELO.)
Front section.
  (To CLAYBORN.)
Sports.
  (To GROOVE.)
Any final words, brother Groove?

GROOVE
  (Composing at some point the OTHERS might
  hum/harmonize April In Paris behind him.)
I'll always remember my participation and believe me, I

ain't lying, when the North End Preservation Association went to young Thomas' to do some signifying.

T. Mims ain't trying to be meddle-some, though young Thomas may object, we built a visual symposium because his loyalties are suspect. Is he is with us, or is he a-in't he may be with us or he may-n't. It's hard to detect.

Now we didn't built the pit to start no shit, or put nothing in the game, it's just so the boy won't forget, the roots from whence he came.

T. Mims christened the pit and we think it's good 'cause he named it in honor of the lamented Fleetwood. At a monument it might not seem enough, and yet, being as he was a black man in America?,

it's the only damn monument he's liable to get.

OTHERS
(congratulate GROOVE.*)*

T. MIMS
There being nothing else to say, I hereby suggest the adjournment of the North End Preservation Association, suburban session.

TUPELO
Let it be.

GROOVE
Done. — Gentlemen, until tomorrow morning. Usual place, usual time.

CLAYBORN
Guaranteed.

GROOVE
Just time for my chauffeur to get me to school to pick up little master Langston.

T. MIMS
You ought to bring little Langston to a meeting. Never too

young to start.

GROOVE
You know, I've been thinking that very same thing myself.

(To TUPELO.*)*
To school, James.

TUPELO
You the boss, Boss.

T. MIMS
(To GROOVE.*)*
Don't forget to call Joyce.

(GROOVE & TUPELO *exit.*)

CLAYBORN
Well, we left him a sign.

T. MIMS
Don't know how he's going to take it.

CLAYBORN
I'd pay money to see his wife's face.

(Exiting.)
Come on man, let's go see if we can find some of them pills they was talking about.

T. MIMS
I think he passed the audition.

(Surveys scene. To audience.)
And that's what we do.

(Calling after CLAYBORN.*)*
You ever hear the one Fleet used to tell about the time he took the Greyhound with this Baptist preacher, a defrocked nun and a cross-eyed bulldog had gas. . .

(*Exits.*
lights down except on bar-b-que pit as we hear the end of April In Paris as Count Basie says "One mo' once."

fade to
**BLACK
& END OF PLAY.**)